WINNING ON THE
INSIDE

CHARLES
STANLEY

OLIVER
NELSON

THOMAS NELSON PUBLISHERS
Nashville

Published in Nashville, Tennessee, by Thomas Nelson, Inc.

ISBN 0-7852-7285-2

Printed in the United States of America
3 4 5 6 HDC 03 02 01 00

CONTENTS

INTRODUCTION

FACING
TEMPTATION

When you hear the term *temptation,* what flashes into your mind? What pictures and emotions does this word conjure up in your thinking?

For some, temptation means a delicious hot fudge sundae with whipped cream and nuts dripping off the sides. For others, it's the man or woman who has become the focus of secret fantasies at the office. For the teenager, the word may bring to mind a can of beer or a pack of cigarettes or a member of the opposite sex who has been declared off-limits by parents.

To what does *your* imagination turn when you think of temptation?

This is a very important question as we begin a study on this topic. In a sense, whatever comes to mind is what this book is about. Our concern is not with *what* tempts us, but with *who* tempts us and how we are to respond to temptation.

For many people, the prospects of overcoming temptation seem slim. They say, "I've tried and failed so many times before. Why frustrate myself all over again?"

There are several reasons we must never give up in our struggle against temptation.

First, if you fail to engage in a struggle against temptation, a defeating habit in your life will take root and rob you of your confidence in the power of God in your life. You will feel disheartened and may even come to believe that God does not love you or that He has abandoned you in your struggles in life. At that point, you are in danger of developing what the Bible calls a "hard heart."

A hard heart develops when people hear the truth, believe the truth, but refuse to apply the truth. It is a process that occurs over time, but a process that nonetheless follows a fairly predictable pattern: a Christian recognizes sin in his life, feels convicted about it, does nothing about it, and becomes less sensitive to the prompting of the Holy Spirit. At the point where the person feels no conviction at all over a particular sin, he becomes callous and begins to "quench" the work of the Holy Spirit in his life (see 1 Thess. 5:19). That is a very dangerous position to be in.

The person who develops a hard heart is a person who loses all moral and ethical direction, insofar as the Holy Spirit is concerned. To be adrift, without a moral compass, is a highly unsatisfying way to live. It truly is a life without meaningful reward.

A failure to fight against temptation can lead to a great gulf of separation from God. The pattern is evident in countless lives. When we refuse to confront temptation and struggle against it, we begin to cut ourselves off from the spiritual lifeline of God's power in our lives. God loves us still. God remains available to us. But *we* have turned away from God so that He no longer can work in us and through us to the extent He desires.

Second, if you refuse to engage in a battle against the temptation to sin and you lose confidence in God's power and presence in your life, you will be hesitant to offer Christ as the answer to others who are controlled by sin. Your witness for Christ will be deeply impacted. One of the immediate results of being set free from a controlling habit is the desire to share with others the power of God that has set you free. Satan loves to keep us in bondage to sin because our potential for the kingdom of God is greatly diminished.

Third, if you fail to engage in a battle against temptation to commit one type of sin, you likely will find yourself more prone to engage in still other types of sin. We've all heard the phrase, "One sin leads to another." So often that is the case. Sin is like a cancer in that it spreads. One undealt-with area opens up other areas as well. Once you become accustomed to a particular sin and it becomes entrenched in your lifestyle, it is only a matter of time until other areas become problems.

Fourth, if you fail to engage in a battle against temptation, you ultimately will experience death of some type. James wrote,

> But each one is tempted when he is drawn away by his own desires and enticed. Then, when desire has conceived, it gives birth to sin; and sin, when it is full-grown, brings forth death. Do not be deceived, my beloved brethren. (1:14–16)

James gives us an equation: Temptation + Sin = Death.

Whenever sin manifests itself, some type of death results. Destructive habits take root. The result may be a physical death, usually over time. The sin may bring about a death to a relationship, a death to part of the person's emotional or psychological capacity, a death of reputation, a death of integrity, a death of a career, a death of loyalty or respect. Something is always destroyed when sin is allowed to go unchecked.

If temptation has such deadly consequences, why is it that so many people do not take temptation more seriously?

One of the foremost reasons seems to be that we have excused our failures in the area of temptation by saying, "I'm only human. Nobody's perfect."

There is truth in both statements, of course. The greater truth of God's Word, however, is that although we are human and imperfect, we *are* given free will and therefore, we each have the potential to say no to temptation. We have the ability to confront and overcome temptation as imperfect human beings. The real issue is whether we choose to have the *desire* to overcome temptation.

At the core of our reluctance to confront temptation seems to be a greater issue: pride. We want what we want. We do not want to be conformed to the image of Christ Jesus. We do not want to live in accordance with God's commandments when our own pleasure seems to be at stake. A struggle against temptation requires that we do two things:

1. Choose God's way over our own way.
2. Trust in God to help us succeed in choosing His way.

We'll discuss both of those requirements later in this study, but it is important to recognize at the outset that the struggle against temptation is not a "light" issue. It goes to the very core of our spiritual identity.

All of this may sound overly extreme or serious to you. You may be saying, "But my particular problem is not nearly as big as the ones you seem to allude to." If that is the case, great! The best time to deal with temptation is before it takes root in your life and grows into a habit that controls you. As a pastor, I have heard countless stories about how "little" habits turned into bigger ones that resulted in great and widespread devastation. I've heard how marriages, businesses, families, and lives were destroyed, and in tracing back through the "what happened?" and "what caused that?" questions, a very simple action that was contrary to God's plan could nearly always be pinpointed. It may have been only an offhand, careless remark of one spouse to another, a few minutes of looking at pornographic material, the first theft of a few dollars from the company's petty cash, the first drink at a neighborhood bar, the first conversation with a person met at a truck stop. Little temptations *can* become big sins.

As we begin a closer look at the subject of temptation, I want to applaud you for undertaking this study. It takes courage to admit to temptation, to face it, and to defeat it. I have great faith that God will bless you as you engage in this study, and that you will find a new inner strength to overcome temptation and to truly live a victorious life. Winning on the inside is the most important "winning" you can do!

LESSON 1

TAKING A FRESH LOOK AT TEMPTATION

Most people I know believe they have a fairly good grasp of what it means to be tempted. They have felt temptation in their lives. They also know in their minds the right response to temptation: say no! Most people I know want to say no to temptation.

But . . . most people I know also admit that they frequently give in to temptation, and they bear guilt about doing so. What these people do not know, in part, is the *whole* of what the Bible has to say about temptation and how to overcome it.

The Bible is not only a book of "do's" and "don'ts," but a book of "how to's." It is an extremely practical book with truth that can be applied directly to daily situations and circumstances. The Bible not only tells us to "yield not" to temptation, but it tells us *how* to avoid yielding and how to avoid tempting circumstances in the first place.

The Bible is also a book of spiritual inspiration. The Bible motivates us, compels us, and encourages us. It gives us the "want to" outlook that we need if we are to overcome temptation. There simply is no better resource book on the temptation to sin and how to overcome temptation than the Holy Bible.

As you begin this study, I encourage you to set aside, to a degree, what you already believe the Bible says on the subject of temptation and inner struggles. As much as possible, approach the Scriptures with fresh spiritual eyes and ears. Let the Bible speak to you in a new way.

Many people have said to me, "I know what the Bible says is true, but I wonder at times if it is really true for *me*. Will God really do for *me* what He has done for others? Can I really trust God for this area of my life today?"

Let me assure you that the Bible *is* for you, and it is for your life right now. God's truth is not bound to any one era or limited to any one classification of person. The truths in God's Word are for all who have accepted Jesus Christ as their Savior and are trusting in God with all their heart, mind, and soul—and the good news is that *every person* is invited to become one of God's people! No promise or principle of God is off-limits to a person's ability to receive it, act upon it, or be conformed to it.

As you study what the Bible says about temptation, I encourage you to go again and again to your own study Bible and to underline phrases, highlight words or verses, and make notes in the margins of your Bible to record the specific ways God speaks to you. I believe in a well-marked Bible, one filled with notes, dates, and insights.

God's truth is for all people at all times, but the application of that truth to your life is always very personal and direct. Take note of the specific ways in which God admonishes, encourages, or directs you.

For Personal or Group Study

This book can be used by you alone or by several people for a small-group study. If you are using this book for a personal

Bible study, you will find places from time to time in which to note your insights or respond to questions. If you are using the book for a small-group study, you may want to use these questions and insight portions for group discussion.

At various times, you will be asked to relate to the material in one of these ways:

- What new insights have you gained?
- Have you ever had a similar experience?
- How do you feel about the material presented?
- In what way do you feel challenged to respond?

Insights

An insight is more than a fact or idea. It is seeing something as if it is new to you. You might consider it an "aha" moment in reading a passage of the Bible—a moment when you say to yourself, "I never saw that before. I've studied this passage for years, but I suddenly have a deeper understanding into what this story or teaching *means*."

Spiritual insights are usually highly individualized and very personal. You may see a new meaning in God's Word because it relates to something you are currently experiencing or have just encountered. At other times, an insight helps you pull together God's truth as you reflect on an experience, relationship, or incident. At still other times, an insight can answer a question for you, give you a sudden knowledge about what to do, how to think, or why you believe what you believe.

Ask the Lord to speak to you personally every time you open His Word. I believe He will be faithful in answering your prayer. I also believe the insights you receive from God will arouse in you an even greater enthusiasm for study of His Word.

Make notes about your insights as you experience them. The more you record insights, the more likely you are to have insights. Time and again, people have told me that the more intentional or focused they were on receiving insights from the Lord, the more they saw new meaning in old, familiar passages. The Bible teaches us this truth, "Seek, and you will find" (Matt. 7:7). As you seek God's meaning, you *will* find it!

From time to time in this book, you will be asked to write what a passage of the Bible is saying to you. These are times for recording your personal response or insight, not for summarizing a group opinion or what someone else in your Bible study group said. Make sure the insight or response is your own.

Experience

Each of us comes to God's Word from a unique background and set of "life experiences." Nobody else in your study group will have exactly your experiences, relationships, or contexts for meaning. Each person has a unique bank of ideas, opinions, and emotions. Therefore, we each have a unique perspective on God's Word.

Differing levels of experience can create problems in group Bible studies, although this is not always the case. People who have gone to church all their lives and have heard the Bible stories and good preaching for many years are likely to have a different depth of understanding of God's Word from that of people who are new Christians or who have never read the Bible. In a group setting, these differences can cause an old-timer to feel impatient and a beginner to feel lost.

What we do have in common are life experiences. We can point to times in which we can say, "Here's how that truth in the Bible displayed itself in my life" or "Here's what happened to me that confirms this truth in God's Word." We each can point to times in which we have been convicted, challenged, encouraged, comforted, or changed by the reading of God's Word.

Of course, our experiences do not make the Bible true. The Bible is truth, period. The importance of relating our experiences to the Bible is this: we discover the many ways in which

God's truth can be applied to human lives and circumstances. We see how God speaks personally and directly to each person. We see how His Word applies to practical needs, questions, and situations. We begin to discover that God's Word is not only universal, but also very specific.

Sharing experiences is vital for spiritual growth. As you share with others, you will find yourself being changed and developed by the Holy Spirit. As others share with you, you will find yourself being encouraged, edified, and instructed by the Holy Spirit. God's intention has always been that His people have vibrant relationships with one another so that the entire body of Christ functions more potently, efficiently, effectively, and with greater compassion. Do not be reluctant to share your experiences. You will grow as a result, and others will benefit.

This is especially important for you to recognize in dealing with the subject of temptation. We often are reluctant to share experiences we have had with temptation because we believe that others will consider us to be "weak" or "a failure." It takes a courageous person to admit to a weakness or failure. It takes a *strong* person to admit to struggles with temptations. The more you share with others about those areas in which you have been tempted and how the Lord has dealt with you and helped you, the stronger you will become in your own ability to withstand temptation, and the more you will encourage others who may have struggled in the same way but were unwilling to admit openly their struggle.

If you are doing this study on your own, I encourage you to find someone with whom you can share your faith experiences. Be open to hearing about that person's faith experiences in return.

Emotional Response

Just as each of us has a personal catalog of life experiences, so each of us has a set of emotional responses. We need to allow others to share their emotional responses to God's Word without judgment or comment. You may be overjoyed or feel encouraged after reading a particular passage in the Bible. Another person may respond to that same passage with fear, perplexity, or doubt. All of these responses are valid ones. There are no invalid emotions.

Face your emotions honestly. Learn to share your emotional responses with others. God made you to be a person with emotions and to use your emotions in productive, godly ways. We find ourselves in trouble only when we deny our emotions, or when we manifest them in ungodly actions.

Temptation is an emotion-laden topic. Very often it is our emotions that open us up to temptation. Certainly our emotions are involved when we yield to temptation. The strong emotion of guilt frequently blankets us after we have yielded to temptation. Joyful emotions associated with God's forgiveness are ones we often feel when we turn to God and confess our sin. Do not back away from the full range of emotions associated with this subject.

One thing we must keep in mind is that our emotional responses do not give validity to the Scriptures. One passage of the Bible is not more "true" than another because we have a stronger emotional response to it. Nor should we trust our emotions as a measuring device for our faith. Your faith must be based on what God says, not on how you feel. The value of taking a look at our emotional responses is one directly related to personal spiritual growth. For example, at times you may not *like* what you read in God's Word. That's an emotional response. Admit to it. Explore *why* you don't like what you are reading. You are likely to be pointed on the road to deeper discoveries about yourself, God's nature, and the relationship God desires to have with you!

In most small-group settings, I have found it much more beneficial for people to express their emotional responses rather than their opinions. Some of the ways in which God speaks to us through His Word are nonverbal. The Holy Spirit often speaks to us in the unspoken language of promptings, intuition, emotions, and deep desires and longings. When we share these feelings with one another, we not only open ourselves to deeper insights into God's Word, but we also grow closer together as members of the body of Christ. A sense of community develops, and we understand more clearly what it means to be "one in the Spirit." Opinions often divide people, but a sharing of emotional responses often pulls people closer together. It is through the sharing of joys and sorrows, assurances and doubts, hopes and fears, that we mature as individuals and as churches.

One of the vital keys to a group study is that you keep in confidence the life experiences and emotional responses, as well as the challenges, that are shared. In a study of temptation, others may admit things that you did not know about their past or present. Those things are not for discussion outside the group. In keeping confidential the experiences and emotions expressed in the group, you will build trust in the group, which in turn will allow for even deeper and more helpful sharing. To break confidence, however, can destroy a group as well as cause serious damage to the one who was vulnerable in sharing.

Challenges

As we read God's Word, we nearly always feel convicted at some point. It is as if God is speaking directly to us.

God's Word may cause you to feel challenged to change something in your life, to take a new step, to make a fresh start, or to have a new resolve. At times you may feel challenged to stand firm or to continue faithfully in the direction you are going. These moments of conviction can be very strong. They may occur once or repeatedly, but they are virtually impossible to escape or ignore.

In the area of temptation, it is very likely that the Lord will speak to you regarding a particular temptation that you are experiencing. Listen closely to what the Lord is saying to you. The word of the Lord to you will never be condemning—it will always be instructive. The Lord will reveal to you what you are to do, but then He will also hold out to you the hope of His presence in you to *help* you do what He tells you to do. The Lord does not instruct us to do anything apart from what He has caused to be written in the Scriptures, and He will not instruct us to do anything that He does not then enable us to do.

The more practical the issues may be in our lives, the stronger the convictions we often feel. Perhaps that is because God's message and meaning are so clear that there is little room to justify, explain away, or misinterpret what God is saying. Allow God's Word to speak to you—don't run from it or hide from it. Do, however, hear the full message from God, including His words of love and support and His directives related to timing and methodology.

I believe we gain a great deal by writing down the ways in which we believe God is stretching us, molding us, calling us, or causing us to believe for more. When we identify clearly and succinctly what God wants us to do and why, we are in a much better position to take action that is measured, deliberate, and responsible. We are called to *respond* to God's Word, not merely to react to it.

Ultimately, God desires to get His Word into us and us into His Word so we can take His Word into the world, live it out, and be witnesses of His Word in all we say and do. We are to be God's living testimony to others that He can enable a person to confront and overcome temptation and to defeat the devil. It is not enough for us to note our insights, recall our past experiences, share our emotions, or write down the ways in which we feel challenged. We must obey God's Word and be doers of it, not hearers only (see James 1:22).

Very specifically, it isn't enough for you to become knowledgeable about temptation or to know all of God's principles and commandments. You must do what God says to do. You are challenged to become a victorious believer, a genuine *winner* over temptation.

Finally, I caution you that as you share your convictions that you be very careful in what you promise publicly to do or vow to God in the presence of others. People often find they feel convicted regarding a particular area of temptation in their lives and they quickly respond, "I promise I will never do that again." Do not make promises or vows lightly. Always put them into the perspective, "with God's help." The key in your life is not in promising to change and then attempting to change on your own, but rather, to put your trust in God and allow Him to work in you and through you to *help* you to overcome the devil.

Keep the Bible Central

I encourage you to guard against the tendency to turn your Bible study on this topic into a type of group "confessional." The intent of this study is not to create a therapy or support group. It is a *Bible* study. Come together for the purpose of feasting on God's Word—to learn from it, to grow into it, to rely upon it. Surely forgiveness can be extended freely to those who may confess sin and seek forgiveness within a group setting. But then quickly return to God's Word as the focus of your time together.

If you are doing a personal Bible study, you also must be diligent in staying focused on God's Word. Self-analysis and introspection are not the goals of this study. Growing into the fullness of the stature of Christ Jesus is the goal!

Prayer

I encourage you to begin and end your Bible study sessions in prayer. Ask God to give you spiritual eyes to see what He wants you to see and spiritual ears to hear what He wants you to hear. Ask Him to reveal to you new insights, to recall to your memory the experiences that are helpful in your growth, and to help you identify your emotions clearly. Be bold and ask Him to reveal to you what He specifically desires for you to take as the next steps in your journey toward becoming a genuine winner over temptation.

As you conclude a time of study, ask the Lord to seal to your heart and mind all that you have learned so that you will never forget it. Ask Him to help you apply what you have learned to daily situations and circumstances. Ask Him to transform you more into the likeness of Christ Jesus—so that you might be as victorious as Jesus in defeating the devil at every turn.

The Depth of God's Word

Avoid the temptation of concluding at the end of your ten-lesson study that you have achieved a total understanding of temptation or that you know all there is to know in order to avoid all temptation. Temptation will come to each of us throughout our lives—perhaps in different forms and in different areas, but it will come nevertheless. Continue on in your reading and study of God's Word. You'll see even more examples of God at work in the lives of His people to help them overcome temptation. Continue to grow and to explore all that God has to say to you about what it means to be victorious over the enemy of your soul. I guarantee you without reservation that as you remain faithful in reading God's Word on a daily basis, you'll have a much greater understanding a year from now about what it means to be whole and to be a winner in Christ Jesus. Grow in God's truth . . . always!

And now as you begin this study, I invite you to consider these questions:

- *What new insights are you hoping to gain about temptation and how to overcome it?*

  _____

  _____

- *In what areas have you struggled with temptation in the past? Is there one specific temptation that you seem to confront repeatedly?*

  _____

  _____

• *How do you feel about temptation and about God's desire that you be victorious over it?*

_____

_____

• *Do you feel challenged to grow in your relationship with the Lord? Do you feel challenged to confront temptation with new resolve?*

_____

_____

LESSON 2

THE BIG PICTURE

One of the most important ways we learn is by a technique that has been likened to a microscope-telescope combination. We at times need to look very closely at something, almost to the point of dissecting it. At other times, we benefit by getting the "big picture" and seeing how details relate or apply to a much larger whole.

In our study of temptation, it is important for us to realize that our individual temptations have a much broader context. You may think that your struggle with temptation does not matter to anybody but you, but it does. Your struggle is not an isolated struggle. Our heavenly Father takes very seriously every victory or defeat in the life of an individual believer, in part because that struggle is part of a much greater struggle.

Let's review in this lesson some of the "big picture" that we all know.

Creation from Chaos

The creation account as we have it in Genesis is a description of God's bringing order out of disorder, creation out of chaos.

> In the beginning God created the heavens and the earth. The earth was *without form, and void; and darkness was on the face of the deep.* And the Spirit of God was hovering over the face of the waters. Then God said, "Let there be light"; and there was light. (Gen. 1:1–3, emphasis added)

The earth was formless, and God gave it form.
The world was in darkness, and God brought forth light.
The world was void of meaning, and God gave it meaning.

The creation of man was the apex of the creation—man was given a very special role to fill:

> Then God said, "Let Us make man in Our image, according to Our likeness; let them have dominion over the fish of the sea, over the birds of the air, and over the cattle, over all the earth and over every creeping thing that creeps on the earth." (Gen. 1:26)

Man was then blessed and told to multiply, fill the earth, and subdue it (see Gen. 1:28). He was given authority over all life—both the plants and the animals.

To ensure that man was equipped for the job of ruling His creation, God gave man the special quality of being created *in God's image,* and *according to God's likeness.* Man, unlike any other part of creation, shared with God an intellect, a will, emotions, an ability to reason and make decisions, and an ability to love, obey, and disobey. All of these are vital to ruling creation the way God desires for it to be governed.

But then Adam and Eve plunged themselves and all of creation into a tailspin by their willful disobedience of God. Both morally and physically, the world was taken back into a state of upheaval.

This disobedience was rooted in Satan's *tempting* Eve and, through her, Adam. So let us ask, "Why was Satan so intent upon tempting Adam and Eve to sin? What was at stake for him?"

The prophets Isaiah and Ezekiel give us brief descriptions of a cosmic war that took place some time before the ordering of the world. According to their accounts, Satan at one time held a very high position in the kingdom of heaven:

> *You were the anointed cherub who covers;*
> *I established you;*
> *You were on the holy mountain of God;*
> *You walked back and forth in the midst of fiery stones.*
> *You were perfect in your ways from the day you were*
> *   created,*
> *Till iniquity was found in you. (Ezek. 28:14–15)*

Satan became filled with pride and decided that he should be God. Isaiah tells us,

> *For you have said in your heart:*
> *"I will ascend into heaven,*
> *I will exalt my throne above the stars of God;*
> *I will also sit on the mount of the congregation*
> *On the farthest sides of the north;*
> *I will ascend above the heights of the clouds,*
> *I will be like the Most High." (14:13–14)*

What followed was a battle that resulted in Satan's being cast out of heaven along with those angels that chose to side with him. Ezekiel tells us that he was cast to the ground—the earth (see 28:17). Satan, a defeated foe in heaven, was allowed to live on this earth.

Why would God allow Satan to live on this earth? His presence here is part of God's provision for the free will given to man. If man did not have the opportunity to disobey or to follow

Satan, man would not truly have free will. Each of us has been given the opportunity to choose whom we will follow and obey.

Satan knows, and has known since man's creation, that to defeat man would be to defeat all of God's creation on this earth. Satan's attack on mankind was simply his way of striking back at God, with an intent of reversing God's process and plunging all of earth back into chaos. Satan seeks revenge against God and a return to the power he once knew—and even more so, he seeks to gain power he never had.

Since the day that Adam and Eve sinned, all of creation has suffered. Paul wrote,

> For the earnest expectation of the creation eagerly waits for the revealing of the sons of God. For the creation was subjected to futility, not willingly, but because of Him who subjected it in hope; because the creation itself also will be delivered from the bondage of corruption into the glorious liberty of the children of God. For we know that the whole creation groans and labors with birth pangs together until now. (Rom. 8:19–22)

- *What new insights do you have into these Scriptures cited? What new insights do you have into your role on the much larger stage of God's eternal plan and purposes?*

_____

_____

Sin Causes Decay and Death

Sin is an agent of decay. Once sin is introduced into anything—an individual, a relationship, a community—order and productivity begin to diminish. Goodness declines.

Evil is not a thing; it is a *lack* of perfection. God's creation was perfect, and evil is a process of reversing that perfection and detracting from it. We can see by looking back over history what resulted when sin was introduced into the world. First, God's order of authority was broken. Man had set himself up to be his own god. We have countless illustrations on all sides that show a perpetual slide from order to disorder, from creation as God intended it to chaos. The battle initiated by Satan continues to rage.

If God had not stepped into history, all of creation might very well have self-destructed. In Genesis 6:5–8 we read,

> Then the LORD saw that the wickedness of man was great in the earth, and that every intent of the thoughts of his heart was only evil continually. And the LORD was sorry that He had made man on the earth, and He was grieved in His heart. So the LORD said, "I will destroy man whom I have created from the face of the earth, both man and beast, creeping thing and birds of the air, for I am sorry that I have made them." But Noah found grace in the eyes of the LORD.

God began again, but the problem of a sin nature in mankind remained. To deal with that problem, God sent Jesus to die for man's sin. Through Christ Jesus, men and women have the opportunity to deal with both the penalty and the power of sin in their lives.

When we come to Christ, God gains a definitive victory over Satan in our lives. Satan has "lost" us and God has "found" us. We are squarely planted on the winning side of eternity.

Up to the point that we accepted Christ as our personal Savior, we experienced many temptations, and we had no certain and lasting means of overcoming those temptations. We had a "bent" to sin, a propensity to sin. Satan was manipulating us to his side.

Once we accepted Christ as our personal Savior and received the Holy Spirit into our lives, we were given a "bent" toward choosing what is right before God. We were given a desire to live our lives in a way that is pleasing and good in God's eyes.

- *In reflecting on your life, in what ways can you see your temptations as part of the larger struggle of Satan to gain your soul and to deny you entrance into the kingdom of God?*

  _____

  _____

- *In looking back at your life, can you identify ways in which you thought about sin differently from the way you think about sin now? Can you identify activities in which you participated freely without even thinking they were sinful, although you now recognize that they were activities contrary to God's commandments?*

  _____

  _____

When a person is truly born again, he will have no desire to sin. He will *want* to do what is right. Furthermore, he will experience a growth in the grace and knowledge of the Lord Jesus Christ. He will be on a path of life—an abundant life now and an eternal life after our physical death.

What the Word Says	What the Word Says to Me
What shall we say then? Shall we continue in sin that grace may abound? Certainly not! How shall we who died to sin live any longer in it? Or do you not know that as many of us as were baptized into Christ Jesus were baptized into His death? Therefore we were buried with Him through baptism into	_____ _____ _____ _____ _____ _____ _____ _____ _____ _____

death, that just as Christ was
raised from the dead by the
glory of the Father, even so we
also should walk in newness of
life. (Rom. 6:1–4)

Grow in the grace and knowledge of our Lord and Savior
Jesus Christ. (2 Peter 3:18)

[Jesus said], "The thief does
not come except to steal, and
to kill, and to destroy. I have
come that they may have life,
and that they may have it more
abundantly." (John 10:10)

[Jesus said of Himself], "Whoever believes in Him should
not perish but have eternal
life." (John 3:15)

A New Process Toward Life

We must be very clear on this point: before an individual
places his trust in Christ, he is in a constantly decaying process.
He is headed for eternal death. However, once an individual
has placed his trust in Christ and has been born anew spiritually, a new process goes into effect. That individual is indwelled
by the Holy Spirit, and the chaotic cycle of sin is reversed into
a cycle that promotes life and results in eternal life. As the
apostle Paul wrote,

> Therefore we do not lose heart. Even though our out-
> ward man is perishing, yet the inward man is being
> renewed day by day. (2 Cor. 4:16)

We are new creatures on the inside. This renewal process is one that enables us to overcome even strong temptations to sin—if we will put our trust in Christ to help us overcome temptation.

Decay happens over time. A total renewal of the inner person also happens over time.

This does not mean that our salvation is uncertain. When a person accepts Jesus as Savior, that person is born anew, and what is "birthed" cannot be unbirthed. The Holy Spirit does not depart from that person. Eternal life is guaranteed to that person—automatically, definitively, and without compromise (see John 3:16).

A holy and righteous life, however, is not automatic. A struggle continues because we still live in physical, earthly bodies that have not been fully redeemed from sin's influence. We must actively seek to put on the new identity in thought, word, and deed that God has ordained for us to have. We must experience a total renewal of our minds and hearts.

What the Word Says

If anyone is in Christ, he is a new creation; old things have passed away; behold, all things have become new. (2 Cor. 5:17)

The inward man is being renewed day by day. (2 Cor. 4:16)

As the truth is in Jesus: that you put off, concerning your former conduct, the old man which grows corrupt according to the deceitful lusts, and be

What the Word Says to Me

----

renewed in the spirit of your
mind, and

----

that you put on the new man
which was created according to
God, in true righteousness and
holiness. (Eph. 4:21–24)

Why Do Satan's Temptations Continue?

Why does Satan continue to tempt us even though we definitively and irrefutably belong to God? For two reasons. First,
if he can't have you, he'll do his best to discourage you and to
make you miserable as long as you live on this earth. Satan
seeks to inflict as much pain and misery as possible. He never
ceases to be an oppressor.

Second, Satan will do his best to keep you from being an
effective witness to others. If he can succeed in making you an
ineffective witness—of destroying your reputation, of causing
you to live under a cloud of guilt and depression, of causing
you to stumble and sin blatantly before others—he has hope
that someone you might otherwise influence will *not* be influenced to accept Jesus Christ as his or her Savior. He knows
that if he can get you caught up in sin—however small it may
be—you are sidelined as far as the kingdom of God is concerned. Every victory Satan has over you is a minor victory in
his thwarting the advancement of God's kingdom.

Our struggle with temptation, therefore, is not limited to
our own selves. It is a struggle that is part of a much greater
struggle between God and Satan and between those who
believe in Jesus Christ and the one who would seek to destroy
them. Paul could not have been any more clear about this than
when he wrote,

> For we do not wrestle against flesh and blood, but
> against principalities, against powers, against the rulers

of the darkness of this age, against spiritual hosts of wickedness in the heavenly places. (Eph. 6:12)

Each one of our struggles has a spiritual core to it. Each battle against temptation—each choice we make for good or for evil—is part of an ongoing struggle between the kingdom of God and the kingdom of Satan. That's the big picture we must keep in mind in our desire to become victorious over temptation. We are not winning for ourselves alone in one isolated incident for one moment on this earth, but our victory is part of a much bigger and eternal victory.

• *What new insights do you have into why temptation exists?*

_____

_____

• *How do you feel about being part of a much bigger struggle between the kingdom of darkness and the kingdom of the living God?*

_____

_____

• *In what ways do you feel challenged in your spirit?*

_____

_____

LESSON 3

WHO'S TO BLAME?

Most of us have no genuine desire to take responsibility for our own temptation. We'd much rather find someone else to blame!

We hear countless stories today of people who attempt to justify their sins by blaming their childhood, their parents, their genetic code, the government, specific circumstances and situations, their employers, and even God. This tendency in us to "pass the buck" is certainly nothing new. It started with the line used by Adam: "The woman whom You gave to be with me, she gave me of the tree, and I ate" (Gen. 3:12). It was perpetuated by the tactic tried by Eve, who said to God: "The serpent deceived me, and I ate" (Gen. 3:13).

Adam tried placing the blame on another person. Eve tried placing the blame on the devil. Neither justification kept Adam and Eve from being accountable for their own actions.

- *As you reflect on your life, what excuses have you attempted to give God for your sin?*

_____

_____

Blaming someone or something else for your particular weakness appears to take the responsibility from your shoulders. But by mentally removing yourself from a position of responsibility, you are also removing yourself from a position wherein you could correct the situation! Until you are willing to take responsibility for your own failures, mistakes, and sins, you will be unwilling, and therefore unable, to do anything about them.

In this lesson, I want to take a look at several of the foremost excuses that people use to justify their weakness in the face of temptation.

"That's Just the Way I Am"

Many people blame their personalities for their inability to deal successfully with particular temptations. They say, "I've always been this way" or "That's just the way I am." The implication in these statements is also, "This is the way I will always be."

In making such a statement, we are actually asking God to take the blame for our sins. We are saying, in effect, "If You hadn't made me this way, God, I wouldn't do this."

The fact is, you *learned* how to sin. You had a built-in propensity or "bent" to sin, but at some point you learned and then *chose* to sin. In most cases, sin has become a bad habit. You do what you do because you have always done what you do. That does not mean, however, that you *must* do what you do or that you cannot change what you do.

God made you with many talents, abilities, dreams, and desires. He expected you to use your innate gifts for His purposes and His glory. He expected you to use all that you are and have for *good*, not evil. Your choice of behavior is just that—*your choice*.

What the Word Says	What the Word Says to Me
For as he thinks in his heart, so is he. (Prov. 23:7)	------------------------------ ------------------------------
Keep your heart with all diligence, For out of it spring the issues of life. (Prov. 4:23)	------------------------------ ------------------------------ ------------------------------
So let each one give as he purposes in his heart. (2 Cor. 9:7)	------------------------------ ------------------------------
Ponder the path of your feet, And let all your ways be established. Do not turn to the right or the left; Remove your foot from evil. (Prov. 4:26–27)	------------------------------ ------------------------------ ------------------------------ ------------------------------ ------------------------------
You are worthy, O Lord, To receive glory and honor and power; For You created all things, And by Your will they exist and were created. (Rev. 4:11)	------------------------------ ------------------------------ ------------------------------ ------------------------------ ------------------------------ ------------------------------

- *For which behavior in your life would you most like to blame somebody else? Is that an indication to you of a particular area of weakness you may have?*

"Everybody Is Doing It"

Many people think that there's safety in numbers—if everybody is engaging in their particular brand of sin, then it must be all right. Nothing could be farther from the truth.

God does not grade on the curve or give in to the popular

wishes of men and women. His commandments and His promises are equally absolute. If God says yes to something, He means yes. If He says no, He means no.

God does not regard peer pressure or group pressure as a justifiable reason for giving in to temptation. Every person is responsible for his or her choices related to God's Word, even if the rest of humanity is in error.

What the Word Says	What the Word Says to Me
[Jesus said], "Enter by the narrow gate; for wide is the gate and broad is the way that leads to destruction, and there are many who go in by it. Because narrow is the gate and difficult is the way which leads to life, and there are few who find it." (Matt. 7:13–14)	_____ _____ _____ _____ _____ _____ _____ _____ _____
So then each of us shall give account of himself to God. (Rom. 14:12)	_____ _____ _____

- *How do you feel about God's challenge to you to go against the tide of sinful humanity and live a righteous life?*

_____

_____

"I Was Talked into It"

More and more people are blaming the influence of others for their behavior, saying such things as, "If it weren't for the people I work with . . ." or "My friend was so persuasive . . ."

This is the same excuse Adam tried to give to God. No matter how persuasive a person may be, in the end you are the one who decides what you will do, when, and to what end. Until you are willing to face up to your personal responsibility regarding temptation and sin, you can change friends, jobs, and even families and still end up being molded and controlled by your environment.

To put the blame for your habits on your circumstances or on other people is to allow someone or something to control your destiny in that particular area. You have handed the direction of your life over to an entity you cannot change and thus cannot control, and which, in the end, will fail.

What the Word Says

[Jesus said], "Beware of false prophets, who come to you in sheep's clothing, but inwardly they are ravenous wolves. You will know them by their fruits. Do men gather grapes from thornbushes or figs from thistles? Even so, every good tree bears good fruit, but a bad tree bears bad fruit. A good tree cannot bear bad fruit, nor can a bad tree bear good fruit. Every tree that does not bear good fruit is cut down and thrown into the fire. Therefore by their fruits you will know them." (Matt. 7:15–20)

For we have spent enough of our past lifetime in doing the will of the Gentiles—when we walked in lewdness, lusts,

What the Word Says to Me

----

drunkenness, revelries, drink-
ing parties, and abominable
idolatries. In regard to these,
they think it strange that you
do not run with them in the
same flood of dissipation,
speaking evil of you. They will
give an account to Him who is
ready to judge the living and
the dead. (1 Peter 4:3–5)

- *In your life, what have you found to be effective in counter-
acting the suggestions of peers to engage in sin?*

_____

_____

"My Family Is Cursed"

We hear a great deal today about generational curses—about
how the sins of the fathers are visited upon their children to
the fourth generation (see Ex. 20:5). A number of people use
this excuse for their weaknesses and sins, saying, "If you knew
the kind of family I grew up in, you would understand why I'm
this way," or "If you had known my father [or mother], you'd
know why I am the way I am."

The good news in this area is that more and more people
are gaining insight into the impact that parents have upon children and how childhood influences can result in adult
behavior. The truth, however, is that this is *not* an excuse for
sin in the eyes of God. Parents and grandparents influence
children, but in the end, children decide what they will *do*.

I was raised in a family situation that was far from ideal, and I
know the weaknesses and propensity for sin that can be woven
into the fabric of a personality from childhood. I understand the
temptation to look to the past as an excuse to allow sin to go

unconfronted or unchecked. But I also know the pain and frustration that such irresponsibility can cause to one's family and friends. I had to make a decision that I was going to leave the past behind and deal with things as they were. It was difficult. Yet it was only after I took responsibility for my actions and asked God to help me change my behavior that I truly was able to make changes. I believe that will be true in your life, too, regardless of how you were raised or what kind of parents you had.

- *In what ways do you believe your parents influenced you to sin? To what degree are you eager to reverse that trend in your family?*

_____

_____

What the Word Says

Fathers shall not be put to death for their children, nor shall children be put to death for their fathers; a person shall be put to death for his own sin. (Deut. 24:16)

For we must all appear before the judgment seat of Christ, that each one may receive the things done in the body, according to what he has done, whether good or bad. (2 Cor. 5:10)

What the Word Says to Me

- *Read Leviticus 20. Notice how many times you find the phrase "His blood shall be upon him" or "They shall bear their sin."*

"This Sin Is Acceptable in My Culture"

There are those who believe strongly that certain sins are acceptable for them because everybody in their immediate neighborhood, social grouping, or cultural setting is engaging in this sin and has engaged in it for generations. This is only an extension of the peer-group and family-inheritance arguments. One's culture can be in error when it comes to the Word of God!

What the Word Says	What the Word Says to Me
One ordinance shall be for you of the assembly and for the stranger who dwells with you, an ordinance forever throughout your generations; as you are, so shall the stranger be before the LORD. One law and one custom shall be for you and for the stranger who dwells with you. (Num. 15:15–16)	_____ _____ _____ _____ _____ _____ _____ _____ _____ _____

"The Devil Made Me Do It"

In recent years, a nationally recognized comedian made popular the phrase, "The devil made me do it." This excuse, however, has been around since Eve.

The truth of God's Word is that the devil has never made any person do *anything* contrary to his or her will. The devil is a deceiver and the father of lies. But the devil's only power over people is through manipulation and deceit. If he could actually make us do things, he wouldn't need to go to the trouble of deceiving us! If Satan could make us sin, the temptation process would be unnecessary. We will deal with the devil's role in the temptation process more fully later, but let it suffice for now that we conclude that the devil cannot *make* us do anything.

What the Word Says	What the Word Says to Me
But I fear, lest somehow, as the serpent deceived Eve by his craftiness, so your minds may be corrupted from the simplicity that is in Christ. (2 Cor. 11:3)	----------------------------- ----------------------------- ----------------------------- ----------------------------- ----------------------------- -----------------------------
He [the devil] was a murderer from the beginning, and does not stand in the truth, because there is no truth in him. When he speaks a lie, he speaks from his own resources, for he is a liar and the father of it. (John 8:44)	----------------------------- ----------------------------- ----------------------------- ----------------------------- ----------------------------- ----------------------------- -----------------------------

"God Led Me into Sin"

Many people come to the conclusion that, because God allowed them to be born into a certain family, put them into association with certain people, or gave them a physical weakness of some type, He has "led" them into sin. The Scripture says clearly that God is not the cause of temptation. James wrote,

> Let no one say when he is tempted, "I am tempted by God"; for God cannot be tempted by evil, nor does He Himself tempt anyone. (1:13)

Look in the Mirror

None of the excuses that we have looked at in this lesson hold water when it comes to justifying our sin before God. The plain and simple truth is that we each are responsible for our own actions and, thus, for our own sin. We have a free will with which we can choose to resist temptation or choose to give in to temptation. The only person to blame for sin is the person we each see in the mirror. As James so clearly stated,

> Each one is tempted when he is drawn away by his own desires and enticed. (1:14)

The decision you must make today is whether you will continue to make these excuses and if you will continue to attempt to "cover" for your own behavior.

Some people believe that if they can't fool God when it comes to their sins, they at least can fool others. That may be true, to an extent and for a limited time. But in the end, you *cannot* fool God and you *must not* fool yourself. Your own eternal destiny is at stake.

- *What insights do you have into the nature of temptation and sin?*

  _____

  _____

- *In what ways are you feeling challenged in your spirit today?*

  _____

  _____

LESSON 4

THE
APPEAL

One of the most frightening passages of Scripture to me is Ephesians 6:11:

> Put on the whole armor of God, that you may be able to stand against the wiles of the devil.

This verse tells me two very important things: first, the devil has a plan that he has tested and perfected. His schemes worked against men such as David, Samson, Peter, Abraham, Jacob, and others. He is a skilled opponent.

Second, the devil is out to destroy every believer. That includes you.

It is of the utmost importance, therefore, that we understand how the devil plans to go about doing his work so that we can resist him. We need to have as much knowledge as possible about his "appeal."

The General Appeals Satan Employs

The first thing we must recognize is that Satan is in the business of deceit. Through his demonic cohorts, he is constantly working to convince us to buy into a lie. His lies are generally aimed at two areas of our humanity: our pride and our need for security.

1. Our pride. From the beginning, Satan tempted mankind to establish an identity apart from God. Think about the implication of Satan's words to Eve:

> Then the serpent said to the woman, "You will not surely die. For God knows that in the day you eat of it your eyes will be opened, and you will be like God, knowing good and evil." So when the woman saw that the tree was good for food, that it was pleasant to the eyes, and a tree desirable to make one wise, she took of its fruit and ate. She also gave to her husband with her, and he ate. (Gen. 3:4–6)

Satan was saying, in effect, "Eve, God has lied to you. You cannot always trust Him to do what is best for you. You need to begin looking out for yourself. It is time to make some decisions on your own and to be your own person. You can be like God. Why serve Him when you can be like Him? Why take care of His stuff when you can have stuff of your own? You don't need Him to take care of you. You can take care of yourself."

The appeal was to the pride resident within us as human beings, that we might abandon the place of significance offered to us by God and establish an identity of independence from God.

- *In reflecting on your life, can you recall an incident in which you were tempted to sin through an appeal to your pride and your desire for independence?*

---

2. Our need for security. Satan often tempts people by appealing to their need for security—that they must accomplish certain goals, possess certain things, be seen with certain people, or be a part of a certain group in order that they might attain emotional, financial, or psychological assurance and security. He tempts us to meet our God-given needs solely through the ingenuity of our minds and physical strength of our bodies, rather than to rely upon God to meet our needs.

Satan tempts us by first feeding us the lie, "If you only had _____" or, "If you only did _____" with the promise, "You would feel more fulfilled as a person, have greater self-confidence, and be more appealing to others."

These two general appeals of Satan work, in part, because we are creatures of free will and are capable of making our own choices. In that, we do have a degree of independence from God and are responsible for our own decisions. We also are responsible to a great degree for *using* the abilities and skills that the Lord has given to us, working to meet our needs as well as contributing to meeting needs in others. What is *not* true, however, is that we can ever be totally independent from God, nor can we totally rely upon ourselves alone for our own provision. Our efforts to do so will not result in fulfillment but, rather, in feelings of frustration, disappointment, and dissatisfaction.

- *In reflecting on your own life, can you recall an incident in which Satan tempted you to sin through an appeal to your need for greater "security" in a particular area of your life?*

Partial truth. Finally, Satan's generalized appeals to us are effective because he never tells the whole story. He never reveals the full outcome. He only gives the introduction to the first chapter of the story—the catchy, appealing "hook." He doesn't tell a person that if he takes a drink, he may end up an alcoholic, or that if she cheats on a test, she may wind up in prison one day for fraud. His appeal is always limited to a narrow, focused, immediate opportunity to engage in sin.

Not telling the *whole* truth about a matter is a lie, and one of the foremost qualities of temptation is that it never deals with the *whole* of any particular situation, circumstance, relationship, or consequence.

An appeal to the senses. Satan's appeals to us are often sensory, based upon our sense perceptions and our physical needs and desires. These things are transitory and are in fluctuation in our lives, and Satan's temptations often come when we are weak or lacking in an area of physical need. The opportunities to yield to sin are also transitory and in fluctuation. But you match up a weakness in a person with a strong opportunity, and the setup is complete for temptation to be most effective.

What the Word Says	What the Word Says to Me
And the world is passing away, and the lust of it; but he who does the will of God abides forever. (1 John 2:17)	_____ _____ _____ _____
I delight in the law of God according to the inward man. But I see another law in my members, warring against the law of my mind, and bringing me into captivity to the law of sin which is in my members. (Rom. 7:22–23)	_____ _____ _____ _____ _____ _____ _____
I know that in me (that is, in my flesh) nothing good dwells. (Rom. 7:18)	_____ _____ _____

- *In your life, can you recall an incident in which you felt tempted to engage in a sinful attitude or activity on the basis of immediate sensory appeal, without any thought to the full consequences of your actions?*

  _____

  _____

- *What new insights do you have into the way Satan tempts?*

  _____

  _____

A Look at Your "Fleshly Desires"

We are not neutral targets for Satan. When Adam and Eve sinned in the Garden, the whole human race was polluted by their sin. Adam's decision to disobey God and to strike out on his own became interwoven into the fabric of humanity. Everybody is born with a propensity to sin. This is why you do not have to teach your children to sin. They are able to figure it out all by themselves!

This built-in mechanism resides in what the Bible calls the "flesh" (see Rom. 7:18). When we become believers, the power of sin is broken, but the presence of sin remains. That means that believers do not have to give in to sinful desires, but those desires will still arise from time to time.

Satan's aim is to get us to satisfy God-given needs and desires in ways that *are outside the boundaries God has set up.* One of the truths we must keep in mind as we combat temptation is that God *has designed a way for our needs to be met.* Our desires are, to a great extent, a reflection of the image of God. We have a desire for love, acceptance, respect, and success. And God has provided a way for us to experience the fulfillment of these desires.

Let's take two examples. We have a desire for food. There is nothing wrong with eating—we must eat to maintain life and health. God provides for us what we need through the bounty of the earth. Satan's temptation, however, is to convince people that they must overeat, eat the wrong things, or starve themselves out of fear of being overweight. His temptations play upon a very real God-given desire, but they are outside the boundaries God has established for health.

Consider the example of sex. Sexual desire is from God with the purpose of establishing a unique relationship between a man and a woman and for the procreation of the human race. God says, "One man for one woman for life." Satan says, "Any man for any woman until you are ready for someone else." God says, "Sex is to be part of the marriage relationship—in that way both the need for sex and the desire for love can be met for all of one's adult life." Satan says, "Sex *is* the relationship, and love is wherever you can find it for the moment." Satan is moving outside the boundaries God has established for the fulfillment of our sexual needs.

The three foremost areas of the flesh in which the devil tempts us are these:

1. *The lust of the flesh.* This area represents our appetites, cravings, desires, hungers. It includes the sexual desire but is not limited to it.

2. *The lust of the eyes.* This includes all those things that spark our desires and appetites, and especially those things that fuel our greed and our perceived need to acquire possessions.

3. *The pride of life.* This refers to anything that promotes or elevates a sense of independence from God—anything that causes us to think we can do our own thing, live our own kind of life, and have it our way. It is especially manifested in our need for power or control, as well as for recognition and praise from others.

What the Word Says	What the Word Says to Me
Do not love the world or the things in the world. If anyone loves the world, the love of the Father is not in him. For all that is in the world—the lust of the flesh, the lust of the eyes, and the pride of life—is not of the Father but is of the world. (1 John 2:15–16)	--------------------------- --------------------------- --------------------------- --------------------------- --------------------------- --------------------------- --------------------------- --------------------------- ---------------------------
Now the works of the flesh are evident, which are: adultery, fornication, uncleanness, lewdness, idolatry, sorcery, hatred, contentions, jealousies, outbursts of wrath, selfish ambitions, dissensions, heresies, envy, murders, drunkenness, revelries, and the like; of which I tell you beforehand, just as I also told you in time past, that those who practice such things will not inherit the kingdom of God. (Gal. 5:19–21)	--------------------------- --------------------------- --------------------------- --------------------------- --------------------------- --------------------------- --------------------------- --------------------------- --------------------------- --------------------------- --------------------------- --------------------------- --------------------------- ---------------------------

Let's take a closer look at how Satan's temptation of Eve involved these three target areas of the flesh.

First, Satan appealed to Eve's pride (the pride of life). His promise was that her eyes would be "opened." Eve came to the conclusion that the tree was "desirable to make one wise." She was convinced that she would have greater insight, knowledge, and understanding. Note that all of these are good things!

Satan also appealed to her desire for power and authority: "you will be like God." Eve knew that she and Adam had already been given a certain amount of authority—more authority seemed like a good thing, also.

Second, Satan appealed to Eve through what she saw (the lust of the eyes). We read that Eve saw that the tree was "pleasant to the eyes." Satan introduced intrigue and curiosity based upon what Eve saw. Her imagination was sparked. She had a desire to touch and possess and partake of what she saw.

Third, Satan appealed to Eve's basic need for food (lust of the flesh). We read that Eve saw that the "tree was good for food." She knew she had to eat—why not eat of *this*?

Do you see the way these three temptations to the flesh are joined together? Rarely does Satan limit himself to one area of the flesh in tempting us. He points out something for us to *notice*—to see, to study, to contemplate. He fills our imagination with a visual image of something desirable.

Satan then gives us a good *physical* reason to seek to act on that visual image, as well as a good *emotional* or *psychological* reason. He will convince us that we "need" to act on what we see.

Consider the example of a teen confronted with his first cigarette. He sees the use of cigarettes in movies and sees magazine and billboard advertisements. Then he sees a pack of cigarettes in the hands of a friend. Satan begins to whisper, "Look." Curiosity is aroused. Satan whispers, "This will make you popular. You'll have more importance in your peer group. And after all, isn't it time you began to make your own adult decisions?" The appeal is to the pride of life. Satan also whispers, "This will also make you calmer and more relaxed. And we all need something to help us cope with stress, right?" The appeal is to a basic lust of the flesh—the need for stress reduction and relaxation. The temptation is complete—all three appeals to the flesh have been made.

- *Can you recall an incident in your life in which you experienced an appeal to all three areas of your flesh: the lust of the flesh, the lust of the eyes, and the pride of life? (It may involve a thing, a person, or an activity.)*

_____

_____

The Element of Doubt

Added to the appeals we have already discussed in this lesson, Satan also introduces an element of doubt. The account of Eve's temptation begins with Satan causing Eve to doubt. Oftentimes, doubt is a major part of the temptation process, and at times, it is the starting point for temptation to take hold.

So many people have come to me through the years with a story that includes lines such as, "If God doesn't want me to _____, then why do I feel the way I do?" or "If this isn't right, why hasn't God put a stop to it?" The element of doubt related to God's goodness, love, forgiveness, provision, or protection is always raised with the use of the word *if*.

The element of doubt generally results in our asking the question: "Why won't God let me fulfill my desire?" This is an extension of the "if" questions. "If God desires for me to succeed, then why won't God let me fulfill my desire?" "If God desires for me to have my sexual needs met, then why won't God let me fulfill my desire?" "If God desires for me to enjoy life and experience peace, then why won't God let me fulfill my desire?" The problem with our asking such if-why questions is that we add the phrase "in the way I desire" so that our question really is, "Why won't God let me fulfill my desire in the way I want to fulfill my desire?"

The real questions we should be asking are these:

- "*When* in God's perfect timing can I fulfill my desires?"

- "*How* would God prefer me to fulfill my desires?"
- "*What* means has God provided for me to deal with my desires in a way that is pleasing to Him while I await His perfect timing and method for complete fulfillment of my desires?"

The truth of God is that He *has* a way for all of our desires to be met. He has a perfect timing, a perfect method, and a perfect "holding pattern" for us to maintain until His timing is right. The question is not whether God wants to meet our needs—the answer to that question is, "He does!" The question we must ask is, "What is God's best provision for meeting my need?"

Doubt takes root in us when we set our eyes on circumstances or situations and we can't see, from our human perspective, how things are going to work out to our advantage. It is then that we often seek to take matters into our own hands. The Lord asks us to trust Him to work things out for us—always for our good—and to keep His commandments as we wait patiently for the fullness of His timing.

What the Word Says	What the Word Says to Me
Doubtless You are our Father . . . You, O LORD, are our Father; Our Redeemer from Everlasting is Your name. (Isa. 63:16)	------------------------------ ------------------------------ ------------------------------ ------------------------------
Blessed are the undefiled in the way, Who walk in the law of the LORD! Blessed are those who keep His testimonies, Who seek Him with the whole heart! They also do no iniquity;	------------------------------ ------------------------------ ------------------------------ ------------------------------ ------------------------------ ------------------------------

They walk in His ways.
You have commanded us
To keep Your precepts diligently.
Oh, that my ways were directed
To keep Your statutes!
Then I would not be ashamed,
When I look into all Your
commandments.
I will praise You with uprightness
of heart,
When I learn Your righteous
judgments.
I will keep Your statutes;
Oh, do not forsake me utterly! (Ps.
119:1–8)

Thus says the LORD, who
makes a way in the sea
And a path through the mighty
waters,
Who brings forth the chariot
and horse,
The army and the power . . .
"Do not remember the former
things,
Nor consider the things of old.
Behold, I will do a new thing,
Now it shall spring forth;
Shall you not know it?
I will even make a road in the
wilderness
And rivers in the desert . . .
To give drink to My people,
My chosen.

This people I have formed for
Myself; They shall declare My
praise." (Isa. 43:16–21)

The Easy, Quick Way

Finally, Satan's appeal to us nearly always provides for our
God-given needs to be met in the easiest, quickest, and least
painful way. Satan offers us an "easy out."

Most of the truly wonderful things in life take both time and
sustained effort to develop and grow. That's true whether it's
a marriage, a friendship, a business, a good habit, a reputation,
a bond of loyalty, a good credit rating, a parent-child relationship, health and fitness, or a ministry to others.

In our desire to avoid the effort and to shorten the time, we
often fall prey to Satan's appeals. He offers a quick fix, an
immediate high, instant gratification.

He also offers us an immediate release from the anxiety that
most people try to avoid. He presents ways for us to experience a "quick release" of built-up tension, frustration, or anger.
At times these solutions can seem in very good order—perhaps
a buyout of a company you have built, a solution that seems
to fit at least a portion of a problem you have.

The question we must ask when "quick solutions" arise is,
"What action on my part would bring God the greatest glory?"
The *action* we must take, however, to determine the answer is
this: we must pray and ask God to make known His will. When
we have God's answer, we will also have peace about a decision. So many sins could be prevented if a person would only
pause to ask, "What do *You* want me to do, Lord? Will this
action on my part bring glory to You?"

God desires for you to live without frustration and anxiety.
But He has also made a way for that to happen. He does not
promise to meet all of our needs immediately. What He promises
is that He will mature us, conform us to the image of Christ

Jesus, and that He will provide for us His peace and inner strength to endure until all of our desires and needs are met.

What the Word Says	What the Word Says to Me
Be anxious for nothing, but in everything by prayer and supplication, with thanksgiving, let your requests be made known to God; and the peace of God, which surpasses all understanding, will guard your hearts and minds through Christ Jesus. (Phil. 4:6–7)	------------------------------ ------------------------------ ------------------------------ ------------------------------ ------------------------------ ------------------------------ ------------------------------ ------------------------------ ------------------------------
[Jesus said], "If you then, being evil, know how to give good gifts to your children, how much more will your Father who is in heaven give good things to those who ask Him! Therefore, whatever you want men to do to you, do also to them, for this is the Law and the Prophets." (Matt. 7:11–12)	------------------------------ ------------------------------ ------------------------------ ------------------------------ ------------------------------ ------------------------------ ------------------------------ ------------------------------ ------------------------------

The good news associated with Satan's appeals is that they are fairly obvious and predictable. Once we are fully aware of how Satan works, we are much better prepared to withstand him. To know one's enemy is truly the first step toward defeating one's enemy.

- *What new insights do you have into the process of temptation and how to withstand Satan's appeals?*

_____

_____

- *In what ways do you feel challenged in your spirit today?*

_____

_____

LESSON 5

OUR
DEFENDER

Satan is on the offense against us always. One of the most important things that you and I must do, therefore, is to have a solid defense against him. Ultimately, our defense is not in ourselves or in any other person or thing. Our defense rests with our Defender, our loving and omnipotent heavenly Father.

You may ask, "Well, if God is our Defender, why does He let the devil tempt us in the first place?"

The reason comes back to free will. God has given man an opportunity to choose.

"But," you may counter, "I've already chosen Jesus as my Savior. Why must I continue to face temptation?" Because it is in withstanding temptation that we are made stronger in our faith and in our witness for the Lord. The Lord, therefore, *allows* Satan to tempt us, for our ultimate benefit, but at the same time, the Lord places limitations on Satan's power to tempt. Temptation becomes something of a "training tool" to cause us to grow up in Christ Jesus.

Will we ever reach the point in our spiritual maturity when we are not tempted? No. The apostle Paul warned us, "Therefore let him who thinks he stands take heed lest he fall" (1 Cor. 10:12). We are each subject to temptation; no person is beyond it because there is always more room for each one of us to grow in Christ and to be conformed to an even greater degree to His character! Even so, we have the knowledge that God will not allow Satan to tempt us to the point where our defeat is assured or that God's purposes are thwarted.

A Limitation on Satan's Temptation

In writing to the Corinthians, the apostle Paul gave a promise concerning temptation. In his promise are two principles that give us insight into God's involvement in our defense against temptation. Paul wrote,

> Therefore let him who thinks he stands take heed lest he fall. No temptation has overtaken you except such as is common to man; but God is faithful, who will not allow you to be tempted beyond what you are able, but with the temptation will also make the way of escape, that you may be able to bear it. (1 Cor. 10:12–13)

God sets several limits on temptation:

1. God limits the intensity of every temptation. God knows you perfectly, inside and out, and He knows how much you can handle. He knows your breaking point. Regardless of the nature of your temptation—be it in the area of finances, sex, anger, or gossip—God knows your limitations. He promises to keep a watchful eye on the pressures Satan brings against you. As you read through the passages of Scripture below, note first that Satan was granted permission to tempt and, second, that a "limit" was set on the amount of pressure that Satan might exert.

What the Word Says	What the Word Says to Me
And the Lord said, "Simon,	-----------------------------

Simon! Indeed, Satan has asked for you, that he may sift you as wheat. But I have prayed for you, that your faith should not fail; and when you have returned to Me, strengthen your brethren."
(Luke 22:31–32)

Now there was a day when the sons of God came to present themselves before the LORD, and Satan also came among them. And the LORD said to Satan, "From where do you come?" So Satan answered the LORD and said, "From going to and fro on the earth, and from walking back and forth on it." Then the LORD said to Satan, "Have you considered My servant Job, that there is none like him on the earth, a blameless and upright man, one who fears God and shuns evil?" So Satan answered the LORD and said, "Does Job fear God for nothing? Have You not made a hedge around him, around his household, and around all that he has on every side?
You have blessed the work of his hands, and his possessions

have increased in the land. But now, stretch out Your hand and touch all that he has, and he will surely curse You to Your face!" And the LORD said to Satan, "Behold, all that he has is in your power; only do not lay a hand on his person." (Job 1:6–12)

Again there was a day when the sons of God came to present themselves before the LORD, and Satan came also among them to present himself before the LORD. And the LORD said to Satan, "From where do you come?" So Satan answered the LORD and said, "From going to and fro on the earth, and from walking back and forth on it." Then the LORD said to Satan, "Have you considered My servant Job, that there is none like him on the earth, a blameless and upright man, one who fears God and shuns evil? And still he holds fast to his integrity, although you incited Me against him, to destroy him without cause." So Satan answered the LORD and said, "Skin for skin! Yes, all that a

man has he will give for his
life. But stretch out Your hand
now, and touch his bone and
his flesh, and he will surely
curse You to Your face!" And
the LORD said to Satan,
"Behold, he is in your hand,
but spare his life." (Job 2:1–6)

- *What overall concluding insights do you have into these passages of Scripture?*

Satan, like all creatures, is subject to God's authority. We often don't think of him in that way. We tend to think of Satan and God on an equal plane, two equal forces pulling in opposite directions. Satan is a fallen angel, a creation of God. He is subject to God's authority.

In placing limitations on our temptation, God assures us of three things:

1. *We will never be tempted more than we can bear*—not in our weakest moments, not even when we are tempted in our weakest area.

2. *God is involved in our struggle against temptation.* He isn't watching from a distance. He is functioning as a referee to the whole situation.

3. *God is faithful.* Even in our darkest hour of temptation, God does not turn His back on us. And no matter how we respond, God remains loyal in His love. In both our victories and defeats, He continues to keep the enemy in check.

- *Can you recall a time when you knew that God had caused a temptation to end "in the nick of time"?*

_____

_____

2. *God designs a way out of every temptation we face.* No temptation situation is hopeless. We are always given a way to avoid falling into sin. Paul wrote that when temptation comes, God "will also make the way of escape, that you may be able to bear it" (1 Cor. 10:13).

Many people are able to anticipate when and where they will face temptation. They can say, "I know that in the situation I'm facing tomorrow, I am going to be tempted to _____." In such cases, you should ask immediately for the Lord to reveal to you how you can escape that temptation! Even if you find yourself suddenly in an extremely tempting situation, you can trust that God has an escape plan for you. Ask Him to reveal it to you, and when He does, act on it.

God will be faithful to provide a way of escape, but we must be faithful to look for it.

- *Can you recall an experience in your life in which God provided an "escape route" for you to take to avoid or to sidestep temptation?*

_____

_____

God Gives Us Power to Overcome

God not only limits our temptations and provides a way of escape, but He also provides us with the power to overcome temptation. Let me quickly share with you three laws related to power:

1. *Power determines potential.* The potential to accomplish any particular task is determined by the power we possess or to which we have access.

2. *Power must be harnessed and applied toward a specific goal before it serves any purpose.* Power in and of itself is useless. Its value lies in its application. The Colorado River, for example, has a great deal of potential power. But it is not until the river comes into contact with the turbines underneath Hoover Dam that the power of the river serves any useful function.

3. *Power, when harnessed and focused, can greatly extend the potential of the one in whose hands the power rests.* Power becomes an extension of the one who controls and directs it. We might say that a lumberjack has enhanced potential when he has a chain saw in his hand—he has greater power to cut down trees and, thus, greater potential to be a successful lumberjack.

With these principles in mind, consider Paul's words to the Ephesians:

> Finally, my brethren, be strong in the Lord and in the power of His might. Put on the whole armor of God, that you may be able to stand against the wiles of the devil. (6:10–11)

Note that the power made available to the Ephesians was not human power. Rather, it was the power of the Lord. Paul encouraged the Ephesians that as they received and used the power of the Lord, *they* would be made strong enough to stand against the devil. Their "potential" for winning against Satan was greatly enhanced.

Paul made this same point to the Romans when he wrote,

Therefore, brethren, we are debtors—not to the flesh, to live according to the flesh. For if you live according to the flesh you will die; but if by the Spirit you put to death the deeds of the body, you will live. For as many as are led by the Spirit of God, these are sons of God. (8:12–14)

Paul was saying, in effect, that we have the power to say no to fleshly desires, but it is a power that is given to us by the Spirit. It is "by the Spirit" that we are to put to death the temptations that arise from our fleshly nature.

In yet a third passage, Paul declared,

For sin shall not have dominion over you, for you are not under law but under grace. (Rom. 6:14)

As believers in Christ Jesus, because the Holy Spirit is resident in us, we have power over sin.

The conclusion we can draw from these three passages of Scripture is a simple but profound one: *believers have a power greater than that of the devil, the flesh, or sin resident in them—it is the power of the Holy Spirit who indwells us when we receive Christ Jesus as our Savior.*

What the Word Says

He [the Holy Spirit] who is in you is greater than he [the devil] who is in the world. (1 John 4:4)

Now this is the confidence that we have in Him, that if we ask anything according to His will, He hears us. And if we know that He hears us, whatever we ask, we know that we have the

What the Word Says to Me

----

petitions that we have asked of   ------------------------------
Him. (1 John 5:14–15)   ------------------------------

You may be saying, "Well, if God has given me all this power, why do I keep giving in to the same temptations over and over? I pray and ask God to help me, but I'm still so weak."

Remember that power must be *harnessed and applied* before it serves any purpose. "Having" the power of God and "using" the power of God are two different things.

James addressed this very issue when he wrote,

> What does it profit, my brethren, if someone says he has faith but does not have works? . . . Do you want to know, O foolish man, that faith without works is dead? (2:14, 20)

James is not diminishing the role of faith—far from it. What he is saying, however, is that faith is useless unless it is applied. It accomplishes nothing unless it is *used* in a practical way for practical outcomes.

In the remaining lessons of this book we are going to focus on practical ways for using our faith to overcome temptation, but let it suffice at this point to conclude: God gives you access to His power, and He desires that you apply His power to overcome temptation. He is your full ally in the war waged against Satan. He makes available to you *all* of His resources. It is as if He has placed in your hands the very weapons you need to succeed in winning a victory over your enemy. He challenges you to pick up those weapons and use them!

- *Recall an experience you have had in which you not only had to "believe" God would help you, but you also had to take a specific action step in order to overcome a temptation to sin.*

Jesus Is Praying for You to Succeed

As a final word of encouragement, let me remind you that Jesus is praying for you that you will succeed in saying no to Satan's lies. We have the strong, active, and constant support of Jesus as our Defender; He is praying for us continually that we will be strengthened and kept safe from the enemy of our souls.

As part of Jesus' prayer for His disciples—a prayer He prayed for them shortly before His arrest in the Garden of Gethsemane—Jesus said,

> I have given them Your word; and the world has hated them because they are not of the world, just as I am not of the world. I do not pray that You should take them out of the world, but that You should keep them from the evil one. They are not of the world, just as I am not of the world. Sanctify them by Your truth. (John 17:14–17)

We know that this prayer also pertains to us because Jesus also prayed that night, "I do not pray for these alone, but also for those who will believe in Me through their word" (John 17:20). That includes you and me!

What a wonderful thing to know that Jesus is praying that we will not be overtaken by Satan. We are in this world for God's ultimate, eternal purposes, and Jesus is praying that those purposes will be accomplished in us and through us until they are fulfilled!

Many people seem to believe that God has somehow let them down or abandoned them when they are tempted. Nowhere does God promise to structure our lives so that we can avoid all temptation. He does, however, promise to help us withstand temptation, to provide a way out, and to keep us from being destroyed by the enemy.

- *How do you feel about the fact that Jesus is praying that you will be kept safe from the evil one?*

  _____

  _____

- *What new insights do you have into the provision of God to help you overcome temptation?*

  _____

  _____

- *In what ways are you feeling challenged today?*

  _____

  _____

LESSON 6

AVOIDING THE DANGER ZONES

Prevention is always the best cure. We know that to be true in many areas of our lives, and certainly it is a principle that extends to temptation. If we can *avoid* a tempting situation, we are wise to do so!

Before we take a look at several "avoidance" tactics, I want to remind you of a central principle of the Bible: you as a believer have been made dead to the power of sin and alive in Christ.

Dead to Sin

The apostle Paul was very candid in describing his battle with sin to the Romans. He wrote,

> For we know that the law is spiritual, but I am carnal, sold under sin. For what I am doing, I do not understand. For what I will to do, that I do not practice; but what I hate, that I do. If, then, I do what I will not to do, I agree with the law that it is good. But now, it is no longer I who do it, but sin that dwells in me . . . I

find then a law, that evil is present with me, the one who wills to do good. (7:14–17, 21)

All of us have experienced what Paul experienced. We know what we should do. At times we even want to do it. Yet we cannot seem to find it within ourselves to do what is right. Unbelievers do not have the power to overcome the power of sin in their lives consistently. For them, it is a futile struggle. For believers, however, it is a different story. Even though Paul readily admitted to the fact of the *struggle,* he also held out the great confidence made available to every believer:

What shall we say then? Shall we continue in sin that grace may abound? Certainly not! How shall we who died to sin live any longer in it? Or do you not know that as many of us as were baptized into Christ Jesus were baptized into His death? (Rom. 6:1–3)

Then a few verses later, Paul writes,

Likewise you also, reckon yourselves to be dead indeed to sin, but alive to God in Christ Jesus our Lord. (6:11)

If the struggle persists, what does Paul mean when he says that as believers in Christ Jesus, we are now "dead" to sin? It means that sin no longer has the power to *force* us to do or think anything. The power of sin still exists as an influence. The power of sin still has access to us, but it does not have any *authority* over us.

Let me give you an example of this. A number of years ago, a friend gave our family a schnauzer puppy. My son, Andy, put a collar on the puppy's neck and proceeded to teach him how to sit down, lie down, and shake hands on command. He did this by saying, "Sit!" and, as he spoke, he pushed the puppy's rear down while yanking his collar up. After repeated similar commands, the puppy would respond to Andy on a verbal command only. The same thing happened with commands to roll over and lie down. Andy started the process of training by giving the verbal command, and then pushing or pulling on the puppy's collar to direct, reinforce, and exert authority for the command.

Satan has a collar around the neck of every unbeliever. When he says, "Act," the unbeliever acts automatically. But when a person becomes a Christian, God removes the collar. Satan can still give the command, but the power of the command to result in action has been broken. The authority behind the command has been negated.

The problem is that many believers don't realize that the collar is off. They continue to respond the same way they responded when they were unbelievers. They don't realize that they can say no, and that the Holy Spirit will enforce their no and give them the power to resist the devil.

- *Are there some temptations in your life that you haven't even thought about resisting because you don't think you are capable of resisting them?*

Alive to Christ

Dying to sin is only half the story. The other half is that we are "alive to God in Christ Jesus our Lord." In accepting Jesus as our personal Savior, we not only had the collar of sin taken from us, but we received the indwelling presence of God to help us. Paul went on to describe our new life further:

> Or do you not know that as many of us as were baptized into Christ Jesus were baptized into His death? Therefore we were buried with Him through baptism into death, that just as Christ was raised from the dead by the glory of the Father, even so we also should walk in newness of life. For if we have been united together in the likeness of His death, certainly we also shall be

in the likeness of His resurrection, knowing this, that
our old man was crucified with Him, that the body of
sin might be done away with, that we should no longer
be slaves of sin. For he who has died has been freed
from sin. (Rom. 6:3–7)

To be baptized, in Paul's time, meant that a person was completely immersed into something, so much so that if a piece of
cloth was "baptized" into dye, the cloth changed color. That's
what happens to us when we accept Christ and are baptized
in Him. Our complete nature changes, our identity changes,
our outward expression changes. We are now indwelled by
Christ and the Holy Spirit is resident within us *to guide us daily
into everything that pertains to our living a victorious Christian life
on this earth and that prepares us for our eternal life with God in
heaven.*

The conclusion we can draw is this: we do not need to say
yes to sin. We are free to say no to temptation. On the other
hand, we must ask the Holy Spirit to act on our behalf and to
help us both *avoid and withstand* evil every time it rises up
against us.

To avoid the danger zones of temptation, we must recognize
first of all that we *can* avoid a great many temptations, and we
can rely on the Holy Spirit to guide us away from tempting circumstances, people, or environments.

- *In your life, do you truly know what it means to be "made
  alive in Christ Jesus"? Have you received Jesus as your personal Savior? Are you trusting in the Holy Spirit to guide
  your life?*

  _____

  _____

God Makes His Wisdom Available

In writing to the Ephesians, Paul identified a number of sins that the believers needed to avoid and he challenged them in saying,

> "Awake, you who sleep,
> Arise from the dead,
> And Christ will give you light."
>
> See then that you walk circumspectly, not as fools but as wise, redeeming the time, because the days are evil. Therefore do not be unwise, but understand what the will of the Lord is. (5:14–17)

Our foremost prayer in avoiding temptation must be, "Lord, give me Your wisdom in how to avoid temptations to sin." The Lord Himself taught us to pray this prayer: "Do not lead us into temptation" (Matt. 6:13). Jesus was saying, "Let us be so led by You, Father, that we won't even come close to temptation."

- *As you reflect on your life, in what areas have you required God's wisdom? Are there some areas in which you seem to need more of God's wisdom than in other areas?*

_____

_____

What the Word Says

If any of you lacks wisdom, let him ask of God, who gives to all liberally and without reproach, and it will be given to him. But let him ask in faith, with no doubting. (James 1:5–6)

For this reason we also, since the day we heard it, do not

What the Word Says to Me

----

cease to pray for you, and to
ask that you may be filled with
the knowledge of His will in all
wisdom and spiritual understanding. (Col. 1:9)

Let the word of Christ dwell in
you richly in all wisdom. (Col.
3:16)

We are to seek God's wisdom in every area of our lives,
including:

1. A careful appraisal of past results. One of the foremost
questions we should ask is, "What happened the last time?"
It may be the last time you associated with a particular person, went to a certain place, or engaged in a certain activity.
We are not wise if we refuse to learn from our past experiences.

2. An understanding of your present weaknesses. We each are
more susceptible to certain temptations given a condition of
weakness we may be experiencing. For example, if we are very
hungry, we can easily be tempted to eat the wrong foods or to
eat too much. If we are very tired, we are more prone to doing
something that will give us a quick boost. People who are committed to walking wisely stay in touch with their feelings,
frustrations, and level of need. Every opportunity, invitation,
and relationship should be evaluated according to one's present state of mind and feelings.

3. A consideration of future plans, goals, and dreams. Many
temptations pale in the light of one's future goals and dreams.
Lying, cheating, stealing, gossiping, sexual sins—virtually all
sins—impact what we will be able to do and the reputation we
will have in the future. The clearer our goals are in Christ Jesus,
the more they can guide us away from sin.

4. A sharp awareness of God's will. Note again that Paul said to
the Ephesians, "Understand what the will of God is."

What Paul meant is this: "Don't go on willfully ignoring what you know in your heart God would have you do. Face up to it!" Paul is calling us to quit playing games, to quit excusing certain things in our lives that lead us into sin, and to quit rationalizing relationships that cause us to stumble. Most people know enough about God's commandments to know right from wrong. They know what God desires for them to do. What they need to do is to remind themselves of what is right and then have the courage to *do* it. Ask God to give you both understanding and courage.

What the Word Says	What the Word Says to Me
Now therefore, thus says the LORD of hosts: "Consider your ways!" (Hag. 1:5)	------------------------------ ------------------------------ ------------------------------
Have mercy on me, O LORD, for I am weak; O LORD, heal me, for my bones are troubled. (Ps. 6:2)	------------------------------ ------------------------------ ------------------------------ ------------------------------
Therefore I also, after I heard of your faith in the Lord Jesus and your love for all the saints, do not cease to give thanks for you, making mention of you in my prayers: that the God of our Lord Jesus Christ, the Father of glory, may give to you the spirit of wisdom and revelation in the knowledge of Him, the eyes of your understanding being enlightened; that you may know what is the hope of His	------------------------------ ------------------------------ ------------------------------ ------------------------------ ------------------------------ ------------------------------ ------------------------------ ------------------------------ ------------------------------ ------------------------------ ------------------------------ ------------------------------ ------------------------------

calling, what are the riches of
the glory of His inheritance in
the saints, and what is the
exceeding greatness of His
power toward us who believe.
(Eph. 1:15–19)

Therefore, since Christ suffered for us in the flesh, arm
yourselves also with the same
mind, for he who has suffered
in the flesh has ceased from
sin, that he no longer should
live the rest of his time in the
flesh for the lusts of men, but
for the will of God. (1 Peter
4:1–2)

[Jesus said], "Whoever does
the will of God is My brother
and My sister and mother."
(Mark 3:35)

Ask the Holy Spirit to Guide You Daily

The Holy Spirit functions much like the supreme "Tour
Guide" of our lives—leading us to the right paths we should
take and directing our attention to the things of God that we
are to do, see, experience, and know. I encourage you to pray
daily, "Holy Spirit, lead me to go where You desire for me to
go, to say what You desire for me to say, and to do what You
desire for me to do. Bring the right people and opportunities
across my path."

The Holy Spirit works within us as the Spirit of truth. He
convicts us of error, cautions us of impending danger, gives us

the ability to discern spirits, reminds us of the words of Jesus Christ, and teaches us *how* to live a life that is pleasing to our heavenly Father. Invite the Holy Spirit to do His work in you! Ask Him to be the Spirit of truth, guiding and directing your every step.

What the Word Says	What the Word Says to Me
[Jesus said], "When the Helper comes, whom I shall send to you from the Father, the Spirit of truth who proceeds from the Father, He will testify of Me. And you also will bear witness, because you have been with Me from the beginning. These things I have spoken to you, that you should not be made to stumble." (John 15:26–16:1)	
[Jesus said], "When He, the Spirit of truth, has come, He will guide you into all truth; for He will not speak on His own authority, but whatever He hears He will speak; and He will tell you things to come." (John 16:13)	

- *What new insights do you have into God's provision for you to overcome temptation?*

_____

_____

• *In what ways are you feeling challenged in your spirit today?*

_____

_____

DRESSED FOR BATTLE

Most Americans are quite fashion conscious. The Bible, however, speaks about a very different kind of wardrobe that we are to wear as believers. It is far more important than the current style! Paul described this spiritual outfit by saying:

> Therefore take up the whole armor of God, that you may be able to withstand in the evil day, and having done all, to stand. Stand therefore, having girded your waist with truth, having put on the breastplate of righteousness, and having shod your feet with the preparation of the gospel of peace; above all, taking the shield of faith with which you will be able to quench all the fiery darts of the wicked one. And take the helmet of salvation, and the sword of the Spirit, which is the word of God. (Eph. 6:13–17)

This is a popular passage among preachers, and through the years, I have found that most Christians are familiar with these verses from Ephesians. I find very few, however, who take seriously Paul's application of these verses. Paul did not say, "Understand the full armor of God," nor did he say, "Research each piece of Roman armor alluded to in these verses." Paul said about this armor, "Put it on!"

Dressed for War

One of the reasons that people fail to overcome temptation is because they are unprepared for Satan's attack. They aren't expecting the devil to come after them in a warlike fashion, with a fierce intensity and intent to kill and destroy.

We've all heard the phrase, "dressed to kill." Paul's variation on that phrase would be that Christians are to be "dressed for war." Most of us never think about dressing for war. And most of us never think about the fact that we *need* to put on the armor of God because we are under attack continually. Paul was very clear in stating, "Put on the whole armor of God, that you may be able to stand against the wiles of the devil" (Eph. 6:11). Our enemy is known. His tactics are known. And the fact that he is continually launching an assault against us should also be known!

In preparing ourselves for war, we must not be like a soldier who has his mind elsewhere in the heat of battle. We must be alert to the task at hand: defeating the devil. We must remain focused on this as one of our prime purposes in life—to confront and defeat Satan on the turf of this earth.

What the Word Says	What the Word Says to Me
For we do not wrestle against flesh and blood, but against principalities, against powers, against the rulers of the darkness of this age, against	------------------------------- ------------------------------- ------------------------------- ------------------------------- -------------------------------

spiritual hosts of wickedness in
the heavenly places.
(Eph. 6:12)

Be sober, be vigilant; because
your adversary the devil walks
about like a roaring lion, seeking whom he may devour.
(1 Peter 5:8)

You therefore must endure
hardship as a good soldier of
Jesus Christ. No one engaged
in warfare entangles himself
with the affairs of this life, that
he may please him who
enlisted him as a soldier.
(2 Tim. 2:3–4)

The Pieces of Our Armor

Before we get into the actual application of the pieces of
armor that Paul described, we need to know what they are:

1. The abdomen covered by a girdle of truth. Roman soldiers wore
a girdlelike belt around their waists. It was actually more like an
apron than a belt. It was made of thick leather, and it covered the
entire abdominal region. It also supported the soldier's sword.

Truth is the foundation for everything else we do as believers. The truth is what gives us hope when we face temptation.
The truth is what allows us to rely fully on God's power as we
face the enemy. It supports what we believe and is the basis for
what we believe. Just as the girdle protects that region of the
body that produces life and is most closely connected to the
movement of God's Spirit within a person, so the truth is what
must govern our lives. It is on the Spirit of truth, the Holy
Spirit, that we rely.

- *Can you recall a time in your life when your "girdle of truth" was missing and you gave in to temptation because you were not following what you knew to be God's truth?*

  _____

  _____

- *What insights do you have into your daily need for God's truth to be manifest in your life?*

  _____

  _____

2. *The chest area covered by a breastplate of righteousness.* Breastplates were usually made of leather, although some of them were studded or covered with metal. The breastplate protected the chest region and, thus, all the vital organs. In the ancient world, men believed the emotions resided somewhere in a person's chest. The breastplate is associated with righteousness because what is right often conflicts with what we feel. The breastplate of righteousness guards us from making decisions based on what we feel rather than what we know to be right. So often temptation begins in our emotions. We must keep our emotions in check so that they are used as God intended for them to be used.

- *Can you recall an incident in your life when your breastplate of righteousness was missing and you yielded to temptation because you acted out of emotion rather than what you knew to be right?*

  _____

  _____

- *What insights do you have into your need for a daily awareness of righteousness?*

  _____

  _____

3. Feet shod with the preparation of the gospel of peace. The foot covering of the Roman soldier was a thick leather sandal wrapped around both the foot and the ankle with leather thongs. The shoe is associated with peace because we are to have peace as our motivation wherever we go, and in our wake, the "footprint" we leave should be one of peace.

* *Can you recall an incident when you yielded to temptation because you did not have peace as your motive?*

_____

_____

* *What insights do you have into the way a person might prepare to be an agent of the gospel of peace?*

_____

_____

4. One hand holding a shield of faith. The shields used by the Roman soldiers were very large. In fact the word translated as "shield" comes from the word that meant "door." Some shields were almost as big as doors. They were made with an iron frame that had leather stretched over it. Some were also covered with metal pieces. A soldier could kneel down behind such a shield and be completely protected in the front. On occasion, the Romans would soak their shields in water so that any flaming arrows that struck them would be extinguished.

Faith is associated with the shield because it is our defense against fear, insecurity, anxiety, and any form of criticism or abuse that might be launched against us from an enemy or persecutor. Faith is our assurance that no matter what a person may say about us or do to us, we are children of God, beloved by God, and redeemed by the blood of Jesus Christ. We do not need to take into our spirit the hurtful remarks of others; we can say in the face of them, "I believe in God and in His Son, Jesus Christ, and all else is only temporary and fleeting."

- *Can you recall an incident when you yielded to temptation because your shield of faith was not up—you were not relying upon the Lord to quench the fiery remarks or deeds of another person?*

_____

_____

- *What new insights do you have into your need for a shield of faith that will cover all your life?*

_____

_____

5. *The head covered with the helmet of salvation.* A helmet was a soldier's most costly and ornate piece of armor. It was designed to protect the entire head.

The mind is where most of our battles are won or lost. It is there that the ultimate decisions about behavior are made, and we "decide" if we will obey or disobey. We are saved from temptation when we choose with our minds to be obedient. Our salvation is what gives us the potential to say yes to God and no to sin. In so doing, we are saved, in a temporal sense, from the act and consequence of sin.

- *Can you recall a time when you yielded to temptation because you willfully chose to sin?*

_____

_____

- *What new insights do you have into your need to remind yourself daily about your own spiritual salvation made possible by Christ Jesus?*

_____

_____

6. *One hand grasping the sword of the Spirit.* This is the only piece of "offensive" weapon that is listed in the armor we are to wear. The Roman sword was more like a dagger, shorter and

broader than a fencing sword. The Word of God is viewed as a sword because of its power to overcome the onslaught of the enemy. We will deal with this more in the next lesson, but for now we should note that the Word of God is what sends Satan and his hosts running for cover.

- *Can you recall a time when you felt at a loss as to what to say to a tempter or to the whispered temptations of the enemy in your mind?*

  _____

  _____

- *What new insights do you have into your need to be reading and meditating on God's Word daily?*

  _____

  _____

No Roman soldier would have dreamed of going into battle without these six pieces of equipment secured and ready for action. To do so would have meant certain death. Paul knew that believers dared not enter into spiritual warfare without being fully prepared as well!

- *How do you feel about these various parts of the armor of God? Is there one part of the armor that you seem to routinely overlook or have difficulty in wearing?*

  _____

  _____

Putting on the Armor

How do we actually put on this spiritual armor? We do it the same way we engage in virtually all spiritual practices that are biblical: we use our faith and our words.

First, you must *believe* that God desires to protect you from the enemy that comes to stalk and defeat you through the tactic of temptation. You must *believe* that Jesus is your full provision. Indeed, He is the One who is your Salvation, the One who gives you peace, the One who imparts righteousness to you, the One who gives you the Spirit of truth, the One who is the object of your faith. You must *believe* that God has given you His Word to use. Putting on the armor of God is putting on a new awareness of Christ Jesus. One person once said, "It's like putting on a new coat of belief, just like putting on a new coat of paint." It is covering your mind and heart again with a full awareness of who Jesus is and what He has done for you. It is coating your mind and heart again with the full awareness of how much God loves you and desires to have close fellowship with you.

Second, you must *state* what it is that you believe. This pattern of confessing or saying what you believe is seen throughout the New Testament. Paul wrote to the Romans, "If you confess with your mouth the Lord Jesus and believe in your heart that God has raised Him from the dead, you will be saved. For with the heart one believes unto righteousness, and with the mouth confession is made unto salvation" (10:9–10).

What we believe establishes our minds. What we actually *say* establishes what will become our behavior—or, in other words, it will become our "stance" in the world. The connection between what we believe and what we say is very important. It dictates what we will eventually do and not do!

How do we *state* the putting on of this armor? Every morning I say the prayer that follows. This may look like a long prayer to you, but you will probably find that it can be said in about three minutes. I encourage you to read this prayer aloud, alone or as a group.

> Good morning, Lord. Thank You for assuring me of victory today if I will follow Your battle plan. By faith I claim victory over _____. [I list some of the things I know I will be facing that day.]

To prepare myself for the battle ahead, by faith I put on the belt of truth. The truth about You, Lord—that You are the sovereign God who knows everything about me, both my strengths and weaknesses. Lord, You know my breaking point and have promised not to allow me to be tempted beyond what I am able to bear. The truth about me, Lord, is that I am a new creature in Christ and have been set free from the power of sin. I am indwelt with the Holy Spirit who will guide me and warn me when danger is near. I am Your child, and nothing can separate me from Your love. The truth is that You have a purpose for me this day—someone to encourage, someone to share with, someone to love.

Next, Lord, I want to put on the breastplate of righteousness. By faith, I strap on this breastplate to guard my heart and emotions. I will not allow my heart to attach itself to anything that is impure. I will not allow my emotions to rule in my decisions. I will set them on what is right and good and just. I will live today by what is true, not by what I feel.

Lord, this morning I put on the sandals of the gospel of peace. I am available to You, Lord. Send me where You will. Guide me to those who need encouragement or physical help of some kind. Use me to solve conflicts wherever they may arise. Make me a calming presence in every circumstance in which You place me. I will not be hurried or rushed, for my schedule is in Your hands. I will not leave a trail of tension and apprehension. I will leave tracks of peace and stability everywhere I go.

I now take up the shield of faith, Lord. My faith is in You and You alone. Apart from You, I can do nothing. With You, I can do all things. No temptation that comes my way can penetrate Your protecting hand. I will not be afraid, for You are going with me throughout this day. When I am tempted, I will claim my victory out loud ahead of time, for You have promised victory to those who walk in obedience to Your Word.

So by faith I claim victory even now because I know there are fiery darts headed my way even as I pray. You already know what they are and have already provided the way of escape.

Lord, by faith I am putting on the helmet of salvation. You know how Satan bombards my mind day and night with evil thoughts, doubt, and fear. I put on this helmet that will protect my mind. I may feel the impact of his attacks, but nothing can penetrate this helmet. I choose to stop every impure and negative thought at the door of my mind. I elect to take every thought captive; I will dwell on nothing but what is good and right and pleasing to You.

Lord, I take up the sword of the Spirit, which is Your Word. Thank You for the precious gift of Your Word. It is strong and powerful and able to defeat even the strongest of Satan's onslaughts. Your Word says that I am not under obligation to the flesh to obey its lusts. Your Word says that I am free from the power of sin. Your Word says that He that is in me is greater than he that is in the world. So by faith I take up the strong and powerful sword of the Spirit, which is able to defend me in time of attack, comfort me in time of sorrow, teach me in time of meditation, and prevail against the power of the enemy on behalf of others who need the truth to set them free.

So, Lord, I go now rejoicing that You have chosen me to represent You to this lost and dying world. May others see Jesus in me, and may Satan and his hosts shudder as Your power is made manifest in me. In Jesus' name I pray, Amen.

You may choose to pray the whole armor of God onto your life in different words, but this is a sample of *how* such a statement of belief can be made in prayer.

You may say, "But aren't you just psyching yourself up for the day?" My response is, "Exactly!" However, I am *not* psyching myself up by telling myself a bunch of lies about myself. I am speaking the truth about who Jesus is and what God has promised to do for me. I am reminding myself what I believe. I am setting my mind and heart toward the "right path" setting for the day ahead.

Something happens when we *state* our beliefs. We grow stronger inside. We have a greater resolve. We have an increased motivation.

- *How do you feel when you state aloud what you believe to be true about the Lord Jesus and the power of God made available to you?*

_____

_____

Putting First Things First

I can't imagine going out to preach without having on my socks or a shirt. I make sure I am properly dressed *before* I step into a pulpit. The time to put on spiritual armor is *before* you encounter temptation, not after temptation comes.

Furthermore, Paul did not *suggest* that we put on the whole armor of God. He *commanded* the believers to do so. He knew that even one missing piece of armor puts a person at a disadvantage that could cost him or her an important spiritual victory.

No matter *how* you choose to put on the spiritual armor of God, you will do so by your faith and by your verbal and vocal confession of what you believe. Do so as a top priority! Make this one of the first things you do every day. It worked for Paul. I know it has worked in my life. I am confident it will make a difference in your life as you seek to win victories over temptation.

- *What new insights do you have into God's provision for us to overcome temptation?*

_____

_____

- *What new insights do you have into the concept of "the whole armor of God"?*

  _____

  _____

- *In what ways do you feel challenged in your spirit today?*

  _____

  _____

LESSON 8

WIELDING THE SWORD

My favorite hobby is photography. An ideal vacation to me is loading up all my camera equipment and taking off for a couple of weeks on a photographic safari. In my endeavor to increase my skills as a photographer, I have learned some important lessons. One of them is that there are no problems unique to me as a photographer. Regardless of the questions I have or the predicaments I find myself in, some other photographer has already wrestled with the same dilemma. I have also learned that the best way to save myself hours of headache is to ask a pro how he deals with a problem.

In applying this same approach to temptation, we are wise to ask, "Who has struggled with the same problem and dealt with it successfully as well as consistently?" The answer is given by the writer of Hebrews:

> For we do not have a High Priest who cannot sympathize with our weaknesses, but was in all points tempted as we are, yet without sin. (4:15)

If we are looking for an expert who has had experience with temptation and has overcome it successfully, we need to look no farther than Jesus! He is the master pro in this area. The foremost incident we have of Christ's temptation is in Matthew 4.

Matthew set the stage for us by saying, "Then Jesus was led up by the Spirit into the wilderness to be tempted by the devil. And when He had fasted forty days and forty nights, afterward He was hungry" (4:1–2).

Jesus had withdrawn into a wilderness area, led by the Spirit. He had fasted, which was a custom associated with prayer. For one month and ten days, Jesus had gone without food in the course of His intense prayer. At the end of forty days and forty nights, He was "hungry." Most of us would say we were "starving" at that point! But Jesus was not only hungry for food. He no doubt was weak physically from not having eaten. He was no doubt drained emotionally from His prolonged time in prayer. All of His physical and emotional energy would have been at a low ebb. We have mentioned in previous lessons the importance of recognizing that temptations often come to us when we are feeling "low" physically or emotionally. Well, if there was ever a time to tempt the Lord Jesus, that was it. And Satan knew it.

It is doubtful that any of us will ever come to a more vulnerable position than Jesus was in when the tempter came to Him in the wilderness.

The Ultimate Temptation

Matthew tells us,

> Now when the tempter came to Him, he said, "If You are the Son of God, command that these stones become bread."
> But He answered and said, "It is written, 'Man shall not live by bread alone, but by every word that proceeds from the mouth of God.'"
> Then the devil took Him up into the holy city, set

Him on the pinnacle of the temple, and said to Him, "If You are the Son of God, throw Yourself down. For it is written: 'He shall give His angels charge over you,' and 'In their hands they shall bear you up, / Lest you dash your foot against a stone.'"

Jesus said to him, "It is written again, 'You shall not tempt the LORD your God.'"

Again, the devil took Him up on an exceedingly high mountain, and showed Him all the kingdoms of the world and their glory. And he said to Him, "All these things I will give You if You will fall down and worship me."

Then Jesus said to him, "Away with you, Satan! For it is written, 'You shall worship the LORD your God, and Him only you shall serve.'"

Then the devil left Him, and behold, angels came and ministered to Him. (4:3–11)

- *What new insights do you have into this passage of Scripture?*

_____

_____

I hope you will have noticed two things from this passage.

1. Jesus did not make one original comment during the entire interaction He had with the tempter. This is amazing to me. The Son of God—the One who knows all things and has the power to do all things, the One whose words we study, memorize, and meditate on—chose to respond to temptation using the truth of His Father's Word. The three passages that Jesus quoted were from God's Law in the Old Testament (see Deut. 8:3; 6:16; and 6:14).

2. Jesus' use of the Word of God was effective. The plain truth of God's Word directed at the deception behind each of Satan's enticements was enough. No creative arguments were required. No fancy mental footwork was involved. Jesus simply quoted the Word of God back to Satan, and that was enough to cause Satan to withdraw from Him.

These two truths evident in this passage are very liberating to me. They mean that I don't have to outsmart Satan. I don't have to discuss things with him. I don't even have to muster up enough raw willpower to fight Satan. I simply have to know the Word of God and then to speak it to him. That's something I can do—and that every person can do!

- *How do you feel about the fact that quoting the Word of God was sufficient for resisting the tempter?*

———————————————————————————

———————————————————————————

The Power of the Word of God

There are four primary reasons that a well-chosen passage or verse of Scripture is so effective against temptation.

1. God's Word exposes the sinfulness of what you are being tempted to do. One of Satan's subtle snares is to convince you that what you are being tempted to do is not really a sin. Satan has a smooth way of rationalizing sin away. When we turn to the Word of God for an answer to Satan, we are confronted with the *truth*. In the natural, there was nothing wrong with Jesus needing bread or desiring bread. After all, He had been without food for forty days. What was wrong was for Jesus to take matters into His own hands on the basis of His personal needs. He was saying back to Satan through the verse that He quoted, "My ultimate responsibility is not simply to satisfy My physical needs, but to obey My Father in heaven." The truth of God's Word exposed the sinfulness of what Satan was requesting.

The same thing will happen when we turn to the Word of God for an answer to Satan's temptations. You will see clearly what is at stake. God's Word takes you right to the heart of the matter and allows you to see things for what they really are.

- *Can you recall an incident in your life, or in that of someone else, in which you were tempted to sin because an argument seemed so rational? What from the Word of God would have refuted that argument?*

———————————————————————————

———————————————————————————

2. God's Word gives God's objective viewpoint on the situation. The Scriptures provide us a divine perspective. So often we will say to a friend, "Give me your objective opinion." Well, if we want a truly *good* objective opinion, we need to look to the Word of God. That's where we get God's perspective.

Too often we can get caught up in the strong, emotional feelings we have that make us vulnerable to temptation. The truth of Scripture pulls us away from our runaway emotions to a position of objectivity.

What the Word Says	What the Word Says to Me
Oh, how I love Your law!	------------------------------
It is my meditation all the day.	------------------------------
You, through Your command-	------------------------------
ments, make me wiser than	------------------------------
my enemies;	------------------------------
For they are ever with me.	------------------------------
I have more understanding	------------------------------
than all my teachers,	------------------------------
For Your testimonies are my	------------------------------
meditation.	------------------------------
I understand more than the	------------------------------
ancients,	------------------------------
Because I keep Your precepts.	------------------------------
I have restrained my feet from	------------------------------
every evil way, That I may keep	------------------------------
Your word.	------------------------------
I have not departed	------------------------------

from Your judgments,	-----------------------------
For You Yourself have taught	-----------------------------
me.	-----------------------------
How sweet are Your words to	-----------------------------
my taste,	-----------------------------
Sweeter than honey to my	-----------------------------
mouth!	-----------------------------
Through Your precepts I get	-----------------------------
understanding;	-----------------------------
Therefore I hate every false	-----------------------------
way.	-----------------------------
Your word is a lamp to my feet	-----------------------------
And a light to my path.	-----------------------------
(Ps. 119:97–105)	-----------------------------

3. God's Word causes us to focus our minds. It is impossible *not* to think about something. Stop reading for a moment, and try your best not to think about pink elephants. You won't be able to do it. I have planted that idea, and you will at some point have at least a fleeting image of a pink elephant in your mind! We are thinking all the time, and we cannot avoid thinking. What we each must do, therefore, is to focus our attention on those things that are good to think about!

One of the surest ways to head temptation off at the pass is to turn your thoughts toward God's Word the first moment that a temptation enters your mind. Eve's biggest mistake was talking things over with Satan. She should have repeated back to him verbatim what God had commanded her to do and then just walked away.

What the Word Says	**What the Word Says to Me**
Finally, brethren, whatever	-----------------------------
things are true, whatever things	-----------------------------

are noble, whatever things are
just,
whatever things are pure,
whatever things are lovely,
whatever things are of good
report, if there is any virtue
and if there is anything praise-
worthy—meditate on these
things. (Phil. 4:8)

Set your mind on things above,
not on things on the earth.
(Col. 3:2)

4. *When we voice God's Word, we are activating our faith.* When we turn to God's Word and quote it to Satan, we are actually pulling the "on" switch for our faith. As we discussed in the previous lesson, there is a dynamic connection between what we believe and what we say and a direct connection between what we say and what we do. Our faith is ignited—what we believe takes on life and power—when we *speak* God's Word to the tempter. Nothing moves God like the active faith of His people.

What the Word Says	What the Word Says to Me
My mouth shall speak wisdom, And the meditation of my heart shall give understanding. (Ps. 49:3)	
My tongue shall speak of Your word, For all Your commandments are righteousness. (Ps. 119:172)	

Building Up an Arsenal

To be able to speak the Word of God to the tempter, one must first *know* the Word of God. In the moment of temptation is not the time to go running for a concordance or a Bible index to find an appropriate Scripture. We must have the Word of God resident in us. We must *memorize* God's Word so that we have key verses ready and waiting should temptation arise. These verses are like arrows in a quiver—they are the gleam and glint on the Sword of the Spirit, the Word of God (see Eph. 6:17).

I know Christians who spend hours figuring out crossword puzzles, but they declare they don't have time to study the Word of God. I also know Christians who know dozens of phone numbers off the top of their head, but they contend it is too hard to memorize the Scriptures. Ask God to help you become more disciplined in your reading and memorizing of the Bible, and then begin to take action.

To combat the onslaughts of the enemy effectively, you need an arsenal of verses on the tip of your tongue—verses that are so familiar they come to your mind without any conscious effort on your part.

What the Word Says	What the Word Says to Me
My son, if you receive my words,	------------------------------
And treasure my commands within you,	------------------------------
So that you incline your ear to wisdom,	------------------------------
And apply your heart to understanding;	------------------------------
Yes, if you cry out for discernment,	------------------------------
And lift up your voice for understanding,	------------------------------

If you seek her as silver,
And search for her as for hid-
den treasures;
Then you will understand the
fear of the LORD,
And find the knowledge of
God.
For the LORD gives wisdom;
From His mouth come knowl-
edge and understanding;
He stores up sound wisdom
for the upright;
He is a shield to those who
walk uprightly;
He guards the paths of justice,
And preserves the way of His
saints.
Then you will understand
righteousness and justice,
Equity and every good path.
(Prov. 2:1–9)

When wisdom enters your
heart,
And knowledge is pleasant to
your soul,
Discretion will preserve you;
Understanding will keep you,
To deliver you from the way of
evil,
From the man who speaks per-
verse things,
From those who leave the
paths of uprightness

To walk in the ways of
darkness . . .
To deliver you from the
immoral woman,
From the seductress who flatters with her words . . .
So you may walk in the way of
goodness,
And keep to the paths of righteousness.
For the upright will dwell in
the land,
And the blameless will remain
in it;
But the wicked will be cut off
from the earth,
And the unfaithful will be
uprooted from it.
(Prov. 2:10–13, 16, 20–22)

There are several areas in which I encourage you to seek out
a verse that seems to speak in a special way to you. Once you
find that verse, memorize it. Find a verse that:

- *Deals specifically with the area in which you are most
  often tempted.* If you recognize that you are most
  prone to lying, cheating, giving in to anger—whatever the area of temptation that grieves you
  most—find a verse that speaks God's truth about
  this situation.
- *Addresses the issue of lust.* Men, especially, should have
  several verses on the tips of their tongues that have
  to do with lust or immorality. We all are bombarded

at every turn with the promise of pleasure through illicit sex.

- *Speaks the truth of God about gossip.* It is very easy for each of us to participate in pointless, and at times harmful, chatter about other people.
- *Reminds us of our Christian duty to obey the laws of our government and to respect those in authority over us.*

Let me challenge you right now to take a few minutes to look up these verses and write down the references below:

Area of temptation:

_____

_____

Lust:

_____

_____

Gossip:

_____

_____

Obey laws/respect authority:

_____

_____

Once you have memorized a verse, keep it fresh in your memory by reviewing the verse frequently. Meditate on what the verse means *to you*. Think about specific ways the verse applies to your life. I once heard a story about a young boy who had memorized a great deal of the Bible, but this young boy was also caught stealing money from the church offering plate. When the pastor confronted the boy, he began by quoting him a verse on stealing. The boy quickly pointed out that the pastor had slightly misquoted the verse, but he failed to see any connection between the verse and his behavior. Memorizing Scripture isn't enough. You must see how it relates to your personal life!

The Renewal of Your Mind

The process of filling your mind and heart with Scripture is one that the Bible refers to as the "renewal" of the mind. Paul wrote to the Romans:

> Do not be conformed to this world, but be trans-formed by the renewing of your mind, that you may prove what is that good and acceptable and perfect will of God. (12:2)

Each of us wants to know what God considers to be *good.* Each of us wants in our heart of hearts to engage in what God considers to be *acceptable* behavior. Every Christian I know wants ultimately to do the will of God that will bring that person into greater wholeness and fulfillment in life—which is the *perfect* will of God. The way to discover what God desires for us, and then actually to begin to walk in that way and to engage in the activities that God desires, is to read and study God's Word and to do so with such regularity, focus, memorization, and meditation that the Scriptures *become* the way we think.

We have referred in several places in this study book to the strong connection among what we believe, say, and do. That link not only flows from belief to speech to action, it also flows from action to speech to belief. What we do reinforces the meaning of what we say, and what we say reinforces to our own minds what we believe. A positive cycle is created that results in a genuine transformation of our minds.

- *What new insights do you have into the provision of God for overcoming temptation?*

_____

_____

- *In what ways are you feeling challenged in your spirit?*

_____

_____

***

I recognize that some of you who are studying this topic may not have access to a Bible concordance. Let me recommend several verses to you to help you locate the verses that you need to have in your arsenal. Consider these a starting point only!

Any temptation that seems unbearable	1 Corinthians 10:13
The temptation to gossip	James 1:26
The temptation to lust	Psalm 119:9 Proverbs 6:24–33 Galatians 6:7–8 Colossians 3:2–3
The temptation to fear	Psalm 56:3 John 14:1
The temptation to think you are getting away with sin	2 Corinthians 5:10 Galatians 6:7–8
Troubled by circumstances	John 16:33
The temptation to get involved with debatable things	2 Corinthians 5:9
The temptation not to do the wise thing	Ephesians 5:15–16
The temptation not to obey parents	Ephesians 6:1–3

The temptation to demand your own way	1 Corinthians 6:19–20
The temptation to do things that will harm your body	1 Corinthians 6:19–20

LESSON 9

NO LONE RANGERS

One of the great truths of the Christian faith is that God never intended for any of us to function as spiritual lone rangers. Not only does He desire for us to develop a personal relationship with Him through His Son, Jesus Christ, but God also desires that we be in close association with other believers in Christ who will build us up, admonish us at times, and befriend us always.

The final stage in developing a strong self-defense against temptation is *accountability* to others.

Accountability is a willingness to provide an explanation of one's activities, conduct, and fulfillment of assigned responsibilities. Each of us is accountable to someone in some way. On the job, we are accountable to our employers or a board of some kind. In our communities, we are accountable to the government in the way we keep its laws. Children are accountable to their parents, and when they are in school, they are accountable to their teachers.

Morally and ethically, we are accountable first to God and, second, to the entire body of Christ.

Many people balk at this, saying, "My moral conduct is nobody's business. That's between the Lord and me." But is it really?

We have mistakenly come to believe that since we have a personal relationship with God, who promises to help us when we are tempted, we should omit any mention of that aspect of our lives from the rest of our relationships. Temptation is a private thing, after all. But as private as temptation may be, *sin rarely is private*. Sin eventually reaches out beyond the confines of an individual life and touches others around it. Even those things that you consider to be "only in your mind," will eventually influence the way you think, speak, and act to others. The question is not *if* a so-called private sin will become public, but rather who is going to find out and when.

- *To whom do you consider yourself to be accountable for various aspects of your life?*

  _____

  _____

- *How do you feel about accountability to others in the body of Christ?*

  _____

  _____

An Effective Deterrent

When we are in close affiliation with other believers, we have an effective deterrent against temptation and sin for several reasons:

1. We have an outlet for talking about the feelings and frustrations that may lead us to yield to sin. Talking about our inner feelings often keeps a person from acting on his feelings. This outlet may be temporary, but in many instances, a temporary "bandage" is enough to get people from where they are to the point where they are willing to probe the root issues of the problem they are experiencing.

I am convinced that many extramarital affairs I have heard about in counseling sessions through the years had little or nothing to do with sex. Pressures at home and work had built up to the point where one or both spouses were so concerned about their own problems and needs that they failed to communicate and to spend time *talking and listening* to each other with compassionate hearts.

- *In your life, have you experienced benefit in avoiding sin by talking to someone about your feelings or problems?*

_____

_____

2. We have someone who shares our belief in Christ Jesus who will pray for us. When you are part of a group of believers who are accountable to one another, you have a built-in support system of those who will help you in your battles.

- *In your life, have you experienced benefit in standing strong against temptation through praying with someone or asking someone to pray for you? Are you aware of others who may have interceded on your behalf to keep you from sin?*

_____

_____

3. We quickly discover as we share with others that we are not alone in our temptation. As cited in a previous lesson, the apostle Paul made this point in 1 Corinthians 10:13 by saying, "No temptation has overtaken you except such as is common to man." Knowing that you are not alone in your temptation relieves some of the pressure.

- *In your life, have you had an experience in which you shared a problem with someone only to discover that you were not alone in either your problem or how you felt about it?*

_____

_____

4. We find that we have a source of wise counsel. Often the experience of others can provide us with great insight about how to approach a particular temptation. Pooling the wisdom and creativity of a concerned group of fellow believers always gives birth to new ideas and solutions. You likely have discovered this as you have worked within your current small group on this topic of temptation. Those who are "accountability partners" have the advantage of objectivity and fresh insight. They may also bring to your attention key verses of Scripture that you had not thought to explore or to memorize previously.

At times, the wise counsel of a group may come in the form of practical information a person had not previously encountered or facts that had been in some way hidden from the person. A woman in a church I once pastored was married only a short time when she discovered her husband was involved in a homosexual relationship. She told me that after she and her husband divorced, several of her friends came to her and said that they knew he was involved in homosexuality before their wedding. She said, "I asked them why they didn't tell me. They said, 'We didn't think it was any of our business.'" Her friends were dead wrong. They violated a scriptural principle of sharing the truth with someone in order to help that person. We *are* our brother's keepers. This does not mean that we have a right to become nosy and seek out every bit of information about every person. It does mean that when we have information that would be helpful to a person who we know is making a decision, entering into a marriage, embarking on a business relationship or venture, and so forth, we should be willing to share that information freely.

The warnings and admonitions that we give to others must be given in a spirit of love and help, never in a desire for manipulation, but they should be given openly and freely as opportunities arise in the course of your "accountability partnership" with one another.

What the Word Says	What the Word Says to Me
Brethren, if a man is overtaken in any trespass, you who are spiritual restore such a one in a spirit of gentleness, considering yourself lest you also be tempted. Bear one another's burdens, and so fulfill the law of Christ. For if anyone thinks himself to be something, when he is nothing, he deceives himself. (Gal. 6:1–3)	_____ _____ _____ _____ _____ _____ _____ _____ _____ _____
Open rebuke is better Than love carefully concealed. Faithful are the wounds of a friend, But the kisses of an enemy are deceitful. (Prov. 27:5–6)	_____ _____ _____ _____ _____
Let the word of Christ dwell in you richly in all wisdom, teaching and admonishing one another in psalms and hymns and spiritual songs. (Col. 3:16)	_____ _____ _____ _____
Now I myself am confident	_____

concerning you, my brethren,
that you also are full of goodness, filled with all knowledge,
able also to admonish one
another. (Rom. 15:14)

He who rebukes a man will
find more favor afterward
Than he who flatters with the
tongue. (Prov. 28:23)

- *In what ways have others helped you to live a godly life—
  either by admonishing you against sin or encouraging you to
  act righteously?*

- *What new insights do you have into the role we are to play
  in one another's lives as members of the body of Christ?*

Choosing an Accountability Partner

The Bible does not give us any rules that govern when and
how often we should meet with other believers for "accountability" purposes. I have observed a number of accountability
groups over the years. My daughter, Becky, had a person with
whom she met once a month and, in between meetings, they
stayed in touch by phone. My son, Andy, met with his accountability partner once a week over breakfast. One pastor on our
staff met with an accountability group once a week. Some of
the teenagers in our church meet during lunch at school.

Accountability partners don't necessarily have to have for-
mal meetings. They do need to discuss their lives with one

another on a periodic basis and be willing to discuss openly all issues and subjects.

You likely will find that your best accountability partner will be a person with whom you have something in common. It should be someone of your same sex. It should be someone you respect spiritually. This does not mean that your partner needs to be a Bible scholar or pastor, but, rather, your accountability partner should be someone who is seeking to gain God's perspective on life and truly wants to develop personally in keeping with God's desires.

One thing you do *not* want to have is a relationship with someone who criticizes you every time you get together. Neither do you want someone who will never confront you. A balance needs to be struck between encouragement and exhortation or instruction, with far more encouragement than exhortation. I suggest that you and your partner or group make a decision never to give opinions unless asked for them. And then be free in asking for opinions!

Many people who function as accountability partners have never thought of themselves in this way. They simply see themselves as good Christian friends. That's the way it should be!

No person in the body of Christ should be a "Lone Ranger." Even the Lone Ranger needed Tonto! We each need someone who will know us and whom we cannot deceive. We each need someone who will accept us as we are and yet challenge us to become more like Christ. We each need a friend on whom we can depend fully.

Ask God to bring such a person into your life if you do not presently have such a friend. If you do have such a friend, be open to ways in which you might deepen your friendship and hold each other to even greater degrees of accountability.

What the Word Says	What the Word Says to Me
A man who has friends must himself be friendly,	------------------------------ ------------------------------

But there is a friend who sticks
closer than a brother. (Prov.
18:24)

Therefore comfort each other
and edify one another, just as
you also are doing. (1 Thess.
5:11)

- *What new insights do you have into the plan of God for you
  to overcome temptation?*

  _____

  _____

- *In what ways are you feeling challenged in your spirit?*

  _____

  _____

LESSON 10

MISUNDERSTANDINGS ABOUT TEMPTATION

In my years of pastoral work, I repeatedly have encountered six theories regarding temptation, none of which can be supported biblically but all of which seem to enjoy widespread belief. These misunderstandings cause many well-meaning believers to live under a burden God never intended them to bear. Consequently, they become discouraged and unmotivated. Each is a distortion of the truth, and therefore I believe Satan is the source of these misunderstandings.

In Paul's writings to the Corinthians, he pointed out that ignorance of Satan's schemes allows Satan to take advantage of believers (see 2 Cor. 2:11). I believe that a misunderstanding in the area of temptation does just that. It sets up a person to be deceived and to become discouraged.

We'll take a look at each of these misunderstandings in this final lesson. There will be very few scriptures cited in this lesson for the primary reason that the misunderstandings that we are going to cover do *not* have a basis in Scripture, and therefore they have no scriptural support. We need to be aware of these misunderstandings, however, so that we are not led astray from the truths we have covered in previous lessons.

1. Temptation *Is* a Sin

The first misunderstanding is that it is a sin to be tempted. People who believe this often feel guilty for sins they haven't committed solely on the basis that they have been tempted.

The truth is that we are not responsible for what flashes through our minds. Our responsibility is to control the things that *dominate* our thoughts. Paul clarified this difference to the Corinthians when he wrote,

> For the weapons of our warfare are not carnal but mighty in God for pulling down strongholds, casting down arguments and every high thing that exalts itself against the knowledge of God, bringing every thought into captivity to the obedience of Christ. (2 Cor. 10:4–5)

If God expected us to be able to control what came into our minds in the form of perceptions, fleeting ideas, "notions," creative thoughts, or sensory information, He would not have instructed Paul to write to the believers to "take every thought captive." He would have had Paul write, "Shut the door completely to all thoughts that might be negative." Our responsibility lies in sifting thoughts and in determining which thoughts will be allowed to take root in our minds and hearts. We are to dwell on the good and drive out the bad.

Our environment determines to a great extent what comes into our minds. Even the most cautious people will at some point be exposed visually and audibly to things that will summon ungodly thoughts and feelings. We cannot control what other people wear, say, or do in our proximity at all times. We cannot control what we are invited to participate in (although we obviously can control what we choose to participate in). We cannot control what we accidentally overhear. All of these things are thrust upon us without our consent.

Some of the things we hear pack an emotional punch. And when our feelings get involved, we often become confused. What we need to do is stop and recognize that an emotional response is a natural, God-given gift to us as human beings. It is our responsibility to weigh our emotional response and the external stimuli, and then to determine what sort of action we will take. No sin has taken place until we say or do something in response to stimuli.

One of the ways in which we can know with certainty that it is not a sin to be tempted is the fact that Jesus Himself was tempted, and Jesus never sinned. He was completely righteous, even though He was tempted.

• *Have you ever felt guilty in your life over a thought that came to your mind, even though you did not entertain that thought or act on it in any way? In what ways are you able to let go of that guilt today?*

_____

_____

2. Temptation Ends with Spiritual Maturity

I am always amazed at how people respond when I share that I may be struggling in my personal life. They make an assumption that spiritually mature people are not harassed by temptation. That is certainly not the case.

All of us will face temptation the rest of our lives. There is no escaping it. Somewhere we seem to have acquired the idea that our ultimate goal as Christians is to come to the place in our lives where we are never tempted. Ironically, the very opposite is true. The more godly we become, the more of a threat we become to Satan, and the harder he works to bring us down!

A mark of spiritual maturity is that a person does not sin when faced with temptation, not that a person has no temptations.

- *Have you ever felt guilty over the fact that you still experience temptations? In what ways are you able to let go of that guilt today?*

_____

_____

One of the things we need to realize regarding temptation is that our struggle against it can work something *good* in our lives. Having the temptation is not truly the issue related to spiritual maturity, but rather, what we *do* in the face of the temptation and what we experience as a result of overcoming the temptation.

James wrote:

My brethren, count it all joy when you fall into various trials, knowing that the testing of your faith produces patience. But let patience have its perfect work, that you may be perfect and complete, lacking nothing. (1:2–4)

- *In what ways can you look back over your life and see how your repeated resistance to temptation has made you more patient and stronger in faith?*

_____

_____

3. Temptation Should Cease to Reoccur

A closely related misunderstanding is that once we have dealt with a particular sin or habit, all temptation in that particular area will subside. Again, this misunderstanding is rooted in the concept that Christians can come to the point where they experience no temptations whatsoever.

Often Christians struggle with a particular sin for a long time, even years or decades. They may go through a period when they believe—with evidence supporting their belief—that they have gained a definitive victory over a particular habit, addiction, or problem, and then—WHAM! The old feelings and thoughts come back around.

If this happens to you, I encourage you to check your own Christian disciplines. Have you been reading your Bible and praying daily? Have you remained in close fellowship with other Christian believers? Are you involved in ministry outreaches to people in need or in service to the church? Often old temptations come back during times when a person has been lax in his good spiritual habits. At other times, temptations arise when a person allows himself to become overly tired, under extreme stress, or "burned out." If this is the case, then shore up the area of your defense system that has been breached.

You must also recognize that the Lord has never promised to deliver you from being tempted. He has only promised to help you resist temptation and to overcome it.

If you are tempted time and time again with the same temptation, don't automatically assume that you have a deep, underlying problem. Neither should you assume that you are any more "sinful" than anybody else. Nowhere in Scripture is a person's spirituality judged on the basis of frequency of temptation. The truth is that we are all weaker in some areas than in others. Satan will always seek to capitalize on our weaknesses.

- *Have you ever felt guilty because a very old habit of sin suddenly seemed to crop up as a temptation after years of dormancy? In what ways are you able to let go of that guilt today?*

4. We Simply "Fall" into Temptations

It is not uncommon for me to hear people say, "You know, I was going along just fine, and then suddenly I *fell* into temptation." Such terminology makes it appear that Christians are victims, innocent bystanders, who get swept into sin against their will. That is not the case.

No matter how much pressure we are under, no matter how enticing the temptation, no matter how repeated the temptation, we each have sufficient will to say no and to stand by that no *if we will choose to rely upon the Holy Spirit to help us.*

No Christian falls innocently into sin. The Holy Spirit will convict us every time that we are about to sin or that we have taken the first step toward sinning. We *choose* to sin. In every incident of temptation there is a point at which we cast a deciding ballot either to sin or not to sin.

No person has ever been forced, kicking and screaming against his will, to give in to temptation. We each must face up to the fact that we are personally responsible for our sin and that there is no justification for our sin other than the fact that we *choose to sin.*

- *Have you ever tried to convince yourself that sin just "happened" to you without your will? In what ways are you feeling challenged in your spirit today?*

_____

_____

5. God Is Disappointed in Us When We Are Tempted

I have met people who harbored very strong feelings of guilt over the fact that they were tempted. They felt God was extremely disappointed in them and that He was shaking His head in disgust over the temptations they experienced. My question to them is this, "Do you think God was disappointed in His own Son when He was tempted?" Certainly not. When we feel disappointed in ourselves, or disappointed in something we experience, we often assume that God is disappointed as well. Such, however, is not always the case. God has no expectations that you will be able to live a temptation-free life and, therefore, God cannot be disappointed when you *do* experience temptations. God knows about every temptation that has come your way and will come your way. Nothing takes Him by surprise. Therefore, He does not have any predisposition whatsoever to *ever* be disappointed.

Furthermore, temptation is one of God's tools to develop character and faith in believers, as we noted earlier in citing James 1:2–4. When we are tempted, we have an opportunity to overcome temptation and emerge with stronger faith and character. James also wrote:

> Blessed is the man who endures temptation; for when he has been approved, he will receive the crown of life which the Lord has promised to those who love Him. (1:12)

We are *rewarded* when we resist temptation and persevere through it. The fact that we are tempted does not grieve God; He is grieved only when we give in to temptation.

- *Have you ever felt as if God was disappointed in you because of the temptations you have experienced? In what ways are you able to release that guilt today?*

---

6. It's Possible to Run from All Temptation

Many people believe that if they can just stay away from all sinful environments, all sinful media, and all sinful people, they will be able to live a temptation-free life. I have met people who frequently change jobs, churches, or even move from city to city all in an effort to "escape" temptation. They nearly always end up in a situation very similar to the one they just left. Why? Because they changed their circumstances, but they did not do those things that might renew their own minds.

The territory for temptation is not external. It is internal. Temptation is not waged on a particular geographical or environmental battlefield. It is waged on the battlefield of the mind.

The only way to overcome temptation and to resist the devil is to stand firm in your heart and mind in the midst of temptation.

God has not taken those who believe in Jesus Christ out of this world, but, rather, He calls us to be in this world and to take a stand against evil and for righteousness at every turn. If you spend all of your time trying to avoid temptation, you will become too isolated from society to have any impact on it. There is a time to run and a time to stand!

What the Word Says

[Jesus said], "In the world you will have tribulation; but be of good cheer, I have overcome the world." (John 16:33)

And now, little children, abide in Him, that when He appears, we may have confidence and not be ashamed before Him at His coming. If you know that He is righteous, you know that everyone who practices righteousness is born of Him. (1 John 2:28–29)

What the Word Says to Me

_____
_____
_____
_____

_____
_____
_____
_____
_____
_____
_____
_____

- *What new insights do you have into the nature of temptation?*

  _____

  _____

- *In what ways are you feeling challenged in your spirit today?*

  _____

  _____

CONCLUSION

AND
IF WE
FAIL?

What are we to do if we fail to overcome temptation and actually engage in sin? First, we must confess our sin to God immediately and ask for His forgiveness. Do not say to yourself, "Well, now that I've sinned, I may as well keep sinning." Put an immediate stop to your sin. Go to the Lord and admit, "Lord, I have sinned against You. Please forgive me."

Then, we must receive the Lord's forgiveness by faith and forgive ourselves. We must stop looking at our past and begin to look to our future.

A third step is also important. We must ask the Holy Spirit to help us not to yield to this temptation in the future. We must ask for His help daily as we do the things that we know to do to build a strong self-defense against temptation.

We also must:

- Learn the lessons God desires to teach us in the aftermath of our failure.

- Make amends with any person whom we may have hurt in our sin.
- Be open to sharing with others the dangers of temptation and the consequences of sin, always with a humble heart, a thankfulness for God's forgiveness, and wisdom in knowing what to share and what not to share.

Consider what David prayed:

> *Create in me a clean heart, O God,*
> *And renew a steadfast spirit within me.*
> *Do not cast me away from Your presence,*
> *And do not take Your Holy Spirit from me.*
> *Restore to me the joy of Your salvation,*
> *And uphold me by Your generous Spirit.*
> *Then I will teach transgressors Your ways,*
> *And sinners shall be converted to You. (Ps. 51:10–13)*

Allow God to use your failures to do a transforming work in your life and to draw you into closer intimacy with Him. Allow your failures to create in you an even more intense desire to withstand the devil and to overcome future temptations.

God loves you always. And He always stands ready to forgive and to heal you when you come to Him with a humble heart.